NZ IN A VAN

UK to New Zealand in a
knackered old plumbers van

Simon and Rhona
Wakeling

For Ella-Rose India

CONTENTS

Title Page   1

Copyright   2

Dedication   3

Introduction   9

Preparations   13

The UK to Prague   21

Czech Republic   28

Slovakia & Poland   36

Ukraine   43

Moldova   52

Romania and Bulgaria   60

Turkey   67

Iran   83

Iran–The Dangerous End   103

Pakistan   118

Entering India   131

Nepal   136

Himachal Pradesh   144

Manali to Leh   152

Trapped in Ladakh!   165

The Great Escape!   173

The Scottish Highlands to the Taj   182
Mahal

Rajasthan   192

Bombay (Mumbai)   204

Singapore & Malaysia   214

New Zealand   218

INTRODUCTION

Greetings and Salutations! Welcome to our book about our trip from the UK to New Zealand in an old van! This is based on the blog we wrote in 2008 mainly to keep family and friends updated with where we were. It was also a useful journal to document all the exciting things that happened to us on the way! We'd better start by telling you what we are doing, why, and how! In short, Simon's current career (Recording Engineer and Songwriter) isn't going very well, so instead of persevering with it, he's going to hands-up-and-quit, and re-train to become a pilot which was what he wanted to do since he was a little boy anyway! It seems that New Zealand is as good a place as any to do this (much better than the UK anyway), and as we quite fancy going there

ourselves, we decided to make that our destination of choice. Rhona is a nurse, so she is
planning to get some work to support
Simon (again) though an agency there. Next
up we decided that just 'flying' there was far
too boring (despite said career choice), so as
we normally drive everywhere anyway, we
just thought it would be natural to drive
there....to New Zealand... "What a great
idea" we started congratulating ourselves.
Then we realised that the only possible
route takes us through Iran, which is one of
the hardest countries in the world for westerners to get a visa for, and Pakistan which
is in a state of emergency and is used as a
hide-out by terrorists who commit regular
suicide bombings. We would also have to go
very close to the volatile borders of both
Iraq and Afghanistan and to get anywhere
past India overland, we would have to go
through either Burma (war-torn, and you're
not allowed to drive through it) or Tibet
(rioting separatists). To drive through
Tibet, we would need Chinese residency, a

Chinese driving licence requiring each of us to take a theory test - in Chinese, re-register the vehicle in China and give it Chinese number plates, not to mention all the local permissions. This alone would cost thousands. So the plan at the moment is to get to India from where we will ship the van in a container to Australia, then fly ourselves up to Hong Kong, and make our way down through South East Asia to Singapore via buses, trains and boats, where we will catch a flight to Australia to meet up with our van which will hopefully have arrived! Then we will drive through Australia, and finally, ship the van and fly ourselves to New Zealand to set up more permanent camp. Well, that's the plan anyway. We will be filling in the gaps along the way, and hopefully finding out lots of interesting stuff about the different countries that we travel through, the things going on that we should know about, and some things that we shouldn't know about, so watch this space! Please don't be worried if some time goes by without us posting anything, as we are not taking satellite phones or anything, and chances are, we can't always get internet access. We've put a map up so that you can see our intended route which may well change along the way but it will give you a good idea. Click on it and it'll come up full size. Coming up: the on-going saga that is the van and getting it ready to go! I can't wait!

PREPARATIONS

*Tuesday 12th February
2008, Hastings, UK*

So on 15th February 2008, we bought a 1996 Toyjota Hiace Compact 2.4 Diesel panel van with 98882 miles on the clock for £1550 (in case you are interested... probably not, but we're going to tell you anyway!! haha!). The previous owner in Stevenage assured us that the extremely loud noise coming from the back, which we suspected was the rear diff on the way out, was just the exhaust pipe rubbing on the driveshaft, so he took a couple of hundred quid off, and we bought it... Then the starter motor which worked fine when we test drove it, just stopped working, and we couldn't start it...doh! Not a good start (no pun intended). Well, we got it back to Hastings and to the garage: new starter motor, and as we were previously convinced of otherwise, a new rear diff required... Doh, Doh!! It's gonna cost a grand to fix... At this point, we were starting to have serious misgivings towards the whole trip, but we got the van back and it ended up costing less than half what we were quoted, which was the first bit of good news, and it's been all good from then on in!

The van is great!!!! We have called it "Matatu" due to its resemblance to the 'African mini-bus' that all who have been to Africa know and love! Sweet engine, sweet gearbox ...Yes!... this is going to get us to NZ!!

The next task is to get it ready for our expedition. We need a lot of storage space to carry water, food, spare parts for the van, tools, spare wheels, extra diesel, clothes, other equipment for camping/trekking, a cooler, gas tank and stove, portaloo, a folding bed, solar shower, electric inverter so that we can charge our laptop and other electrics from the vans battery, other cooking equipment, Lonely Planet guide books, and much more!

We started by panelling the walls and floor with plywood and insulating behind it to keep us cool in the heat of mid-summer Asia. We bought a futon for £20 off eBay and bolted it in so that it can swing easily down to make a bed, and be secured safely in the 'sofa' position. What fun!

Many thanks to Dan and Andrea for donating their portaloo and roof rack for our use, and I think it's safe to say abuse!

Saturday, 22nd March 2008

Hey, Rhona here! Si's just off to B&Q and Halfords to get stuff for the Matatu (van). He's desperate to sleep a night in it and I'm afraid that tonight might be the night (wonder if he'll feel the same after a few months in it?). My jobs at the moment are to sell our lovely Peugeot 306, find tenants for our flat, and try to peel off all that plumbers lettering on the side of the van!! - a tedious job I'll tell you. Feels like it's happening now though! My last day at work is the 11th of April, and we've been packing up or selling all our furniture and bits 'n' bobs. I've been getting some job opportunities in New Zealand coming through, which will be handy for when (and if) we get out the other side!

Monday, 14th April 2008

D-day is fast approaching, and things are getting a little scary now. Our flat is almost void of all furniture, and it is starting to hit us that in a couple of weeks we will be homeless, and living in a van... We are already unemployed. Rhona finished her work on Friday, and we have very little time left to organise everything.

So, what's the plan then? Well, we've got this week sorting things out in Hastings, then from Sunday, we are going to spend a week doing a round circuit of the UK. We will drive up to Aberdeen and back to say goodbye to parents and brothers, and to test the van out on home soil. We've then got a few more days in Hastings to iron out any creases before setting off for New Zealand on the 1st of May. We have 4 1/2 months to get to New Zealand before

Simon's pilots' training course starts in September. That is assuming that he gets on the course, it's not been confirmed yet, but will be on the 1st of July.

Talking of the van, it's in the garage again getting all the belts changed, oh and transmission oil is leaking all over the rear wheel hub, and the wipers have stopped working...oooh it'll be fine!!! As far as the rest of it is going, well it's going rather well actually, we have a folding bed, a fridge, worktop, gas hob, portaloo, big water tank, water filter system, storage, blacked-out windows, curtains, roof rack, and an auxiliary power supply consisting of a couple of car batteries linked up to power our kettle and fridge and a few other things. Cool! All we need to do now is cut a hole in the roof (yikes!) to put the spinney roof vent in and we're away! Rhona is still picking letters off the side of the van!

Hey, we had snow in Hastings last Sunday - amazing! Simon thought he would drive the van up a hill to give the new tyres a test, then quickly realised that the hill was quite a bit steeper than originally anticipated when the van started sliding backwards down the hill again!! It was a narrow street with cars parked on both sides, but he somehow managed to miss everything! Oops, close one, we're planning on driving to New Zealand, and it was nearly all over a couple of miles from our house! Let's be a bit more careful next time shall we!

Other exciting news is that we have our Iranian visas stamped in our passports, WAHEY!!! Thanks to Zohreh at Magic Carpet Travel for sorting that out for us, as they are notoriously difficult to get hold of unless you happen to have a sister who is Iranian...nope, not that I know of. We need to make a trip up to London this week to get our Pakistan and India visas stamped in. So it's all starting to happen. Needless to say, we are extremely excited and very reverent of the opportunity to partake in such an outing....?

Until next time...over and out...

Rhona getting to work on the van

THE UK TO PRAGUE

Saturday, 3rd May 2008

"Well Hello, Bonjour, Guten tag!"

As promised, on the 1st of May 2008 at 8:20 in the morning we set off from our empty flat in Hastings UK, and pointed our van in the direction of New Zealand! We got to Dover, and there was a sea in the way, so we drove aboard a ferry for France, and away we went into the great wide world!

The final few weeks were pretty hectic getting things sorted out with our flat and all our belongings, all of which we have now either sold or given away, aside from a van load which we took up to Scotland to put in Rhona's parents' loft! Thanks, Mam and Dad! It really was a last-minute ordeal; we were actually on the phone on the ferry frantic- ally trying to contact all of our house util- ity suppliers to sort out final meter read- ings before our mobile phone signal ran out halfway across the channel!

We did a circuit of the UK a week before we left, which was a great success. The van drove wonderfully all the way up to Aberdeen and back without a hitch. We spent our very first (cold) night in the van in the Yorkshire Dales on the way back, although the van was still so far from liveable. We were so busy with sorting out flat things and tying up loose ends for leaving the country that we didn't do anything else on the van before we left, and we conceded that we would just have to leave with it in a half-finished state. We had tested next to none of the gear on board, but we just stuffed all of our worldly belongings in with Simon's tools, and vowed to sort it out on the way!

I think that with the benefit of hindsight, we were a little ambitious for our first day to try and get through 5 countries from the UK to South Germany including the ferry crossing, but we arrived at a campsite in Saarburg, Germany near the Luxemburg border just as night was drawing, and the rain was setting in. We thought it was a little unfair after having driven all that way, to then have to rifle through the huge piles of our things in the back that had no place to be put away yet, and try to 'organise' them! We just sort of shuffled them around so that we could find some food to eat, get the bed out and go to sleep!

The next morning was very fine though. The plan was to start early and drive to the Czech Republic, but we hung around in the very pretty Saarburg until around 3 o'clock in the afternoon to prioritise sorting the van out. We really enjoyed the village; it was set at the foot of some steep hills and was quite picturesque. When we got up we ventured into town to see if we could find some milk for our Weetabix. But could we find milk anywhere?! We found nearly everything else including delicious bread (which we ended up having for breakfast!), meat, some pretty old, battered apples and bananas... but the only milk they seemed to have was UHT or sterilised! Not happy! Germany is definitely not a place for fruit and veg lovers, but it's great for bread, cheese, and of course all sorts of meat!

We then drove a few hours to near Nurn-berg in South-Eastern Germany. There we spent a night in a forest near the motorway so we could get going early in the morning for Prague. So far we have found most of Europe to be fairly similar, very green landscape, lots of forests and little farming towns. We have spent a lot of time on the motorway so far though and not really explored much as was the plan until we hit the Czech Republic. Si was a little jealous of the cars managing to whiz past us at probably over 120mph on the German motorway which of course has unlimited speed. We managed to hit 80mph a few times in our little van!!

We are now just finishing this post off in Prague whilst having a coffee. Looks like a lovely city in places, but would need a bit more time to explore properly. For now, we are going to head a bit further North East into the mountainous area - Cool! We are planning on barbeque'ing some Czech sausages tonight then go for a hill trek in the

Krkonose Mountains tomorrow. Until then, see ya later. We've included some trivial info for you muse on. Enjoy!

Mileage: 578

Days on the road: 3

Temperature range: 6 to 21 deg C

UK Diesel: £1.20

France diesel: £0.95

Belgium Diesel: £0.95

Luxembourg Diesel: £0.89

Germany Diesel: £1.05

Wild camping in Germany

CZECH REPUBLIC

Tuesday, 6th May 2008

"Dobry den!"

Prague was pretty cool - a bit scummy in the outskirts, but quite beautiful in the centre; lots of gothic looking buildings and bridges alongside a windy river. Great for a romantic get-away. We only had an hour or two in the city, which was kind of spoilt by the amount of time it took us to drive into the central area and find somewhere to park. Once we had found somewhere in a decidedly dubious location, we then spent the rest of the time worrying that the van would get broken into! We could just imagine the next and last post on our blog!

We got out of Prague fairly easily considering that there are only road signs on about one junction in four, and they are all in gibberish to us anyway (look up the Cyrillic alphabet and you'll see what we mean!). To overcome this, we did most of our navigation by map and dashboard compass, so took a bearing on 'Hradek Kralove' which took us most of the way there to

argue on how to pronounce it. We shouldn't
have bothered though, as the last word we
used our combined brain force to decide
on how to pronounce was the Czech word
for 'thank you': 'dekuji'. We decided on a
fairly plain 'der-koo-gee', but it was after
we had said it to about 6 people with varying quizzical reactions that we decided to
ask someone... how embarrassing, it is pro-
nounced completely differently, more like
'ye-ku-ee', so no wonder we got some funny
looks!

I think that so far our main resentment is
that we haven't ever made an effort to learn
more of the world's languages; in the van
coming into the Czech Republic, we managed to remember hello, thank you, 1, 2, 3,
yes and no in Czech, but we're into Slovakia
in a couple of days, and that has a whole new
language, as does every country we visit,
some with many more than one language,
so that has been a little belittling for us. I
think that we were expecting English to be
a bit more widely spoken that our experi-

ence has led us to believe; in fact, no one has spoken any English to us until our fourth day at the campsite in Vrchlabi. Pointing, nodding and smiling stupidly have become quite useful.

Simon loves all the old Skoda's and Fiat's you get in Czech Rep, we think the next trip would have to be buying one of these and driving it home! Si was very temped... Rhona not so sure!! Imagine getting an MOT on one of those things!

The next day we trekked up to 'Sniezka' which is the highest point in the Czech Rep at 1602m. This is part of our side-line attempt to climb higher and higher mountains as our trip goes on. This all started in Arran in Scotland when we climbed Goat Fell at 874m with Rhona's brother Ed and his wife Lydia. We'll see how that goes. We'll maybe end climbing a biggie in Nepal?

It was a beautiful day and the scenery was lovely: plenty of snow still at the top and fairly deserted of people....that is until we nearly reached the top to find that we had gone up the quiet track, and we now joined a paved road going from some huge huts, and going up to more huge huts, restaurants etc. on the top. There were also crowds of people brought up on the chair lifts to walk up the last bit and say they climbed it. That kind of spoilt it a bit. We both felt like we were on some sort of pilgrimage towards the end. We were especially amazed at one girl who was attempting the steep, slippery, snowy ascent in high heels!

From the Czech people that we have met so far, they seem to be a little quiet and grumpy, but then that's what you get for going to Tesco Prague I suppose! There are lots of Lidl supermarkets here as well.

Day five already! We spent the previous night at a campsite near the mountains in a place called Vrchlabi. It was lovely and we were the only campers there. It gave us a chance to have showers (well needed!!), wash clothes and refill our water tank. Unfortunately, we could not use the electric hook-up to recharge all our batteries which would have been nice but not essential. The showers were interesting; they kept going off every few minutes and only stayed hot for about a minute! Hmm, not the best but hey, we ended up clean! We also had breakfast for another £2 each, which was a really lovely continental breakfast.

So after our little re-cooperation, a morning trying to figure out how to dry our washed clothes, a while spent waiting for Rhona to pluck up the courage to give herself her final rabies injection, we headed off again. In hindsight it was a good job there were no onlookers, as the sight of two manky travellers in a campsite injecting themselves with needles may have aroused suspicion!

We headed towards and over the border into Poland for a brief little drive-through. It was again quite different from the Czech Republic. The buildings and houses are very run down, although some are very interesting. Shortly afterwards we were back into the Czech Republic once again to return to our original planned route which was to head on down into Slovakia. We managed to cover quite a lot of ground and found a place to camp at the side of the road just before the Slovakian border. The landscape around the border area is stunning, with vast forested areas and beautiful, large houses built on the sides of rolling hills. Springtime seems to be a good time to visit as well as there are loads of blossom trees all in full flower and fields of yellow rapeseed and little spring flowers!

Mileage: 1244

Days on the road: 6

Temperature range: 3 to 18 deg C

Czech Diesel: 32 Kz (£0.80)

Poland Diesel: £0.90

Climing Sniezka in the Czech Republic

SLOVAKIA &
POLAND

Thursday 8th May 2008

"Ahoj!"

Our Last night in Czech Rep was on quite a high altitude pass between Czech and Slovakia and was a cold one, about 2 or 3 Celsius I think, which for an unheated van is a bit chilly! I'm glad we took Mam's advice and took two blankets and a duvet instead of just one blanket! In the morning we willed ourselves out of bed and headed across the border into Slovakia which is a very beautiful country. Even though it was raining heavily all day, you could get a sense of the majesty of the highest mountain group in the Carpathians. This is where we are headed, the High Tatras, and we arrive at the resort town of 'Stary Smokavec' which is instantly appealing. It's a bit of an out-of-season ski resort but has everything you could want, along with some beautiful old wooden buildings and an old-mixed-with-new feel. Slovakia already seems to be a bit more sophisticated, cleaner and has finer scenery than the Czech Republic. We settled for the night down a quiet countryside road with amazing views of the Tatras.

Our basic routine so far has been to wild camp for two nights, then find a campsite for the 3rd so we can use the showers, washing machine, fill up with water and empty the portaloo etc. It seems to work quite well, as the van recharges itself when we drive (which is quite a lot), and every night we can boil the kettle, charge the laptop etc to our heart's content. The only thing we can't do is run the fridge all night, so the milk gets a bit confused! That reminds me, milk is still very difficult to get hold of around here, ever since Germany, I don't know what the locals have with their Weetabix, but it sure ain't 'cerstve polotucne'!

On Wednesday we climbed up Slavkovsky Stit, which at 2452m is one of the highest mountains in the Tatras and the highest you can climb without being obliged to hire a mountain guide (and without requiring technical climbing skills). It was just perfect mountaineering weather!

It was glorious sunshine all day, and despite layers of sun cream, we still managed to get ourselves burnt! We weren't quite ready for the epicness of this mountain, and we were walking for 9 hours before we got back to the van knackered! It started off being quite hot through the forest at the bottom, then from halfway up, we were wading through patches of waist-deep snow, and the whole top was just capped in deep, crisp unbroken snow. We saw one other person (from a distance) for the whole day, other than that, the whole mountain was ours. It was good to get the crampons on, which Rhona particularly enjoyed as she "just sticks!" The views from the top were amazing, all jagged snowy peaks on one side and open space on the other. What a day! Although it was very tiring! We found a very dubious campsite that night, had showers and went to bed exhausted.

Since we left the UK, we have had quite a lot of rain (storms), indeed it has rained every day apart from the two days that we decided to go out trekking. On those days we had spectacular sunshine all day. How about that!

We had a bit of a change of plan at this stage, and we decided that instead of going through Hungary, Romania, and then Bulgaria as originally planned, it would be far more interesting if we missed out Hungary, and detoured east back into Poland, and into Ukraine, then down into Moldova, getting back on course in Romania again. It would add a little extra distance, but a lot more excitement!

So the following morning we headed off into Poland and towards the Ukrainian border. This will be our first 'proper' border crossing, as so far we have just been driving through EU countries where we could just drive over without stopping. We've heard that it can be very tricky negotiating the Ukrainian border, as the ex-Soviet regime has left behind a legacy of bureaucracy and corruption, and you are certain to be harassed for bribes at every corner (border crossings being the worst!). Moldova is similar, but we have been assured that the murderous separatists are in the east of Moldova, so we won't need to go there.

I think we will start eating out a bit more, as we had a huge slap-up lunch with drinks in a fancy hotel in Poland today and it cost us a total of £7.50. Great, and it's only gonna get cheaper! You've gotta love a bargain!

So for now, at the end of day 8, we are stopped at a beautiful spot, up a steep windy road in southeastern Poland near to the Ukrainian border. Goodnight!

PS. We didn't sleep loads that night, it turns out this very popular spot is used by young couples to have long deep (heated) discussions, and it is used by rowdy men in vans doing whatever they might want to do in a secluded spot in the middle of the night?

Mileage: 1571

Days on the road: 8

Temperature range: 2 to 18 deg C

Diesel: £1

On top of Slavkovsky Stit in Slovakia

UKRAINE

Sunday, 11th May 2008

"Zdrastvuyte!"

Well, the border experience was quite something. We had a couple of hours drive before we arrived at it, so we were there at around 11 am, and the queue was already starting to lengthen. There was an awful lot of waiting before we were ushered in to fill out lots of forms, to be interrogated (in Ukrainian) and have the van searched several times. We had numerous stamps grudgingly placed on a slip of paper by the various officers that we were shuffled between. It was quite a strain, as there was not a common word between us, and we just had to imagine how it must be for a Ukrainian to turn up at the British border control and expect them to speak Ukrainian. Eventually, after three and a half hours of interrogation, we were set free on the Ukrainian side of the border into the unknown.

One thing we realised was that we were not sure if we had got the right insurance for driving a car in Ukraine (no one at the border spoke any English, and they said we had everything we needed; we weren't convinced...), and we were worried about being pulled over and taken to prison. To combat this we have adopted a 'police check avoidance procedure' which involves tailing a truck as we go through a police check so that by the time the police see us it is too late to pull us over! Haha! You laugh, but it has worked so far!

Ukraine seems to be another step poorer than Poland, but there is clearly a lot of hard work going on, and everyone has plantations in their gardens to grow veggies. It seems that everyone in the family from the youngest to the oldest contribute to the farming of crops and looking after the cows, goats, horses or chickens! Rhona particularly loves the horses used for pulling carts and for working the land. It feels a bit like going back in time.

The roads here are consistently bad, no good bits, not many terrible bits, but just bad everywhere, which has made progress a bit slow. We arrived at L'viv by late afternoon and drove straight into town. The entire city centre is cobbled, busy with crazy drivers, and ancient electric trams and electric busses. The old cobbles have been all but destroyed by the cars and lorries that drive over them, and the streets have been made into a big rumble strip, which shook our van like a hungry baby's' rattle. We decided that we didn't have enough time to explore the city fully that day, so we tried to find a hotel to stay in where we could park the van securely, and spend a bit more time exploring the city's old town in the morning. This always seems to take a long time, it was Friday night as well, which meant that there were no rooms anywhere. Eventually, we pulled up outside the fancy four-star 'Hotel Spudnict' with a definite creak to the rear suspension from the battering it had just received from the deranged cobbles. It was a bit more expensive and out of town than we were hoping for, but it was getting late, and we were getting hungry. We splashed out on dinner as well. The food is so different here and you want to try everything. There were lots of pickled meats, fish and vegetables, marinated cabbage, and lots of garlic! The cooked meats were invariably Kyiv-like in style. Still, it barely cost us anything and was pretty good.

Breakfast was another experience with raw fish, hams, salads, pancakes (filled with meat or cottage cheese), meat fritters, but it filled us up for our long day ahead of us. We started our proper tour of L'viv with the hour's walk from our hotel into town and then headed into the old town. We took photos galore, it is so picturesque with many stunning 12th-18th Century buildings (mainly Catholic Churches), and narrow (cobbled of course) streets. A lot of the buildings are in a state of disrepair, but as soon as you go inside one, the detail is just stunning with incredible paintings all over the ceilings and walls, and ornamented golden pillars and cornices, from all different periods of architecture. The city was very important during the 12-16th centuries, being on both the main trade route to the west from Russia, and from Byzantium (Istanbul) to the northern seas. It was a Saturday, and every Church seemed to have a wedding going on. Out in the main city square, there were wedding parties, beautiful dresses, smart grooms and rows of Mercedes wedding carriages everywhere. We thought it was quite surreal. I think we inadvertently gatecrashed a couple of weddings whilst we were looking around some churches just as a bride happened to start walking down the aisle! We thought we were in a wedding comedy film and expected Hugh Grant to appear at any moment! There were a lot of outdoor cafes around the main square, one in which we enjoyed a sandwich for lunch, although I think we have decided that bread is not a Ukrainian speciality!

After lunch, we decided to get back to the van (we were starting to miss it!) and get a couple of hundred miles done towards Kamyanets-Podilskyy which is a fortress town built on a buttress of rock in the middle of a gorge on the way to the Moldovan border. We got lost trying to get out of L'viv, but eventually headed out in the right direction. Navigation is a nightmare here, as all the signs are still in the Cyrillic alphabet, and the maps we have are in our (normal) alphabet, meaning that none of the names tied in together. You have to get to grips with the Cyrillic if you come here! We nearly reached Kamyanets-Podilskyy when we decided to pull over for bed at another beautiful spot down a dirt lane in the middle of the Ukrainian countryside.

The following morning we arose to people walking past us on their way to church in their Sunday best. They all seemed quite suspicious of us two westerners camping and making breakfast in a van parked on the rough trail to their village. We then made our way to Kamyanets-Podilskyy. This city has an old town that was built on a rock island in the middle of what seems to be a convergence of deep limestone gorges. You get to it by going over one of two dizzyingly high bridges which it's possible to bungee jump from if you like (and we saw people rock climbing on the cliffs which looked tempting). At the end of one of the bridges, there is an enormous (and still very complete) fairy-tale castle which you can look around, and go through all the tunnels in the walls, and under the ground. It was so cool! This place is still very un-touristified compared to L'viv (which is meant to be the undiscovered treasure of the east), which was nice, and we enjoyed walking around the old towns' squares and streets. There were more multiple weddings here.

Shortly after lunch, we headed off for the Moldova border an hour or so away.

Mileage: 2055

Days on the road: 11

Temperature range: 6 to 16 deg C

Diesel: £0.60

An old Lada in L'viv, Ukraine

MOLDOVA

Tuesday, 13th May 2008

"Buna!"

The Moldovan border looked deceptively calm when we arrived at it, and all was going well until we got to the last desk - Moldova customs, which was a man who insisted that we fill out all these forms (in Cyrillic Russian) that he knew we wouldn't understand just to be awkward I think. He wouldn't budge, so in the end, we had to get one of the other guards to let us past the gate into the stalls on the Moldovan side, to find someone who spoke English and could help us with the forms. After two trips back and forth from Moldova to correct unsatisfactory entries, the second time coming back with the ladies who were translating for us who also didn't understand what he wanted from us, he smirked, put our forms in an empty drawer, stamped our label and waved us on...

Oh well, we're in Moldova now, and it looks very nice. The roads are cool, bumpy, but wide and deserted. We will see what

Europe's' poorest country has in store for us, but an hour in we get off the main road and settle down for the night. That can wait for tomorrow!

Moldova is a captivatingly interesting place, poorer again than Ukraine, but still, everyone seems to be very busy and working hard...that is apart from the people that work in offices and hotels who have nothing to do! Another interesting thing is that in every village that we went through, each house would have a bench in front of it by the road that the villagers would just sit on, chat, and watch the world (and gawp at us) go by. Every house also has a well outside it, and it's amazing to see all the different colours and styles that people have decorated their wells, from the very basic to the very elaborate with ornate houses built around them! Everywhere you look there are big beautiful horses pulling carts, working the fields, or just tethered at the side of the road chewing grass. A silly thing to say, but they are such a magnificent animal, so much better than oxen or donkeys which you might expect to see in its place. The pace of life seems slower here, everything simpler, and they are very much less accustomed to seeing western tourists. Wherever we are having problems with communication, someone normally manages to find an English speaking family member or villager to rope into translating for us.

I think they knew we were travelling to India when we got to Moldova, as we have just driven through a town called 'Balti', and the word for 'Hello' in Moldovan is 'Buna'! Rhona got them mixed up for a while and kept saying 'Balti' to everyone she met!

We went to visit a monastery overlooking a river that had been carved into the side of a rock cliff by Orthodox monks in the 13th Century. We were the only people there, and the lady in the exhibition centre, with whom French was our most common language, after showing us around all the archaeological finds, told us to go on up to the monastery on the cliff. We didn't quite understand where she was telling us to go, so we just decided to head off in what we thought was the right direction, which took us down all these terrible dirt roads through villages and eventually up to the bell tower on the cliff (which is the only bit of the monastery you can see above ground apart from windows in the cliff face). When we got up there one of the kids from the village playing about the tower came up to us and gave Rhona a bunch of soft grasses that he had been collecting - how sweet! The inside of the monastery was incredible, with sleeping quarters for about 12 monks, a chapel with ornate carvings and artwork, and a door out onto a rock balcony halfway down the cliff draped with rugs and candle stands. Incredible, and all hand-carved out of solid rock

We decided to take refuge that night in a nearby hotel with great views out towards the monastery. It certainly made us laugh; the hotel receptionist didn't speak any English or French, and in fact, didn't really say anything. She kept ushering us to the phone whenever she wanted to tell us something so that her daughter could translate, even when we'd just walked into the room. In all the other countries that we have been through, we've managed to get by using our lonely planet language guide; however, there is no language guide in the Moldova section for some reason!! - not good! We managed to ask for a double room for the night (through her daughter translating on the phone) but turns out you don't get bed sheets and you have to ask for towels. We tried to order lunch, but eventually, she just pointed a dirty finger at one thing on the menu, then shuffled into the kitchen to make it for us which turned out to be lovely chicken noodle soup with bread. When it came to ordering dinner, she once again pointed at something on the menu, and we got the same soup again! - oops!

For breakfast, we were half expecting to get soup again, but she said "omelette", and appeared with 2 fried eggs, slices of cheese, and about a quarter of a sausage each, along with the same stale bread we had the night before, Lovely! Off to Chisinau after that, which is where we now sit posting this blog, so you are completely up to date. Sorry about posting 3 countries at once (don't miss Slovakia and Ukraine below), but it seems as though we are not as skilled at finding internet spots as we thought we might be! Off to Romania this afternoon and yet another language to learn.

Mileage: 2176

Days on the road: 13

Temperature range: 7 to 18 deg C

Diesel: £0.60

Rock-hewn monastry in a cliff in Moldova

ROMANIA AND BULGARIA

Sunday, 18th May 2008

"Buna!"

The border crossing into Romania was a lot quicker than the other two we have encountered, although it must be an inherent characteristic of border guards to be blunt and aggressive. They tend to just shout at you in their language which they must know you don't understand whenever you give them the wrong bit of paper or something.

Romania has even more horses I think than Moldova and is green, hilly and beautiful. There are large parts of Romania that are very mountainous, but unfortunately, we can't go there as we are running behind on schedule if we want to get through Iran before it gets too hot, and to India and Nepal before the serious rainy season start there. So we are going to speed up a bit now and try and get through Romania and Bulgaria quite quickly.

We have had the feeling so far that our presence hasn't been all that welcome in the places that we have been, as people tend to just stare at us and not say anything when we try and talk to them. I think we just need to get to know them a bit better though, as once you've got past the "who on earth are you and what are you driving" stage then they are normally fine. Rhona asked a passing scowling man with a horse and cart if she could take his picture and all of a sudden he just chuckled and got his horses into a fine pose for her saying in Romanian something like: "you want a picture of me? I'm nothing compared to what you look like!". And we all laughed!

We spent one very pleasant night in Romania, with baked beans, corned beef and rice on the menu (hmm lovely...maybe should've stopped at that restaurant we saw after all!). One little stray puppy also enjoyed the shelter under our van..so much so we had to chase him away in the morning for fear of running him over - he was very cute, we would've taken him with us if we could. The next day we spent driving along the coast and over the border into Bulgaria;

our easiest border crossing yet! All the guards spoke English and we were through within 10mins!! Whoopee! At one point just as we were going south of Braila in Romania, the road on the map crossed a very large river which we assumed would be a bridge or something, but we were treated to a very exciting ferry crossing! The ferry was just like a raft about 50cms from the water surface with an engine! All the cars and vans packed on to it overhanging at the edges, and then we chugged across; a highlight. Luckily it was a calm river; we wouldn't have fancied it much otherwise!

We would have liked to have spent more time in Romania than we were able too. Some of the scenery we drove through was beautiful and I think there is a definite cultural richness that we would have liked to tap into a bit more. (I guess that is a common feeling for all the countries we've been through so far and it feels like we're just getting a taster of each for now). Ukraine, Moldova and Romania have made us think about our lifestyle and question "why" do we have the opportunity and resources to be able to go and travel the world when people are slaving away in fields all day just to be able to feed themselves? We have both experienced living in Kenya amidst terrible poverty, but somehow the fact that these are people with the same colour of skin as us, and are a lot closer geographically, has 'struck a chord', so to speak! The nice thing, and perhaps a big difference to what we experienced in parts of Africa, is that people seem to be living very happily, in the rural areas especially. The simplicity of their lifestyle is very appealing although hard work!

So Bulgaria then; well we only had one night here as well (as we were already behind schedule from previous flirtations with Ukraine and Moldova), and we wanted to push through to Turkey the next day. It looks like Bulgaria is going supersonic. Buildings going up everywhere, hotel monstrosities starting to line the coastal areas. Property prices here are soaring as foreigners (Brits) are buying up the villas and houses, and roadside billboards display things like "Brits in Bulgaria" and "Luxury Apartments from 35,000 Euro" (in English of course). The roads here (well the coastal one that we took) are the best since, well Germany, although that's probably just because they are all new.

That said, we can see why; Bulgaria is possibly the most beautiful country we have been to so far. Its' forested mountains are bigger than the Carpathians, the Black Sea is glittering turquoise, the beaches are white and numerous of all sizes and busyness. They have lots of wildlife (we saw wild buffalo by the side of the road, and there are also many bears), and I think I would live here if I could! So I think there is still time - go and buy a house in Bulgaria!!

Mileage: 2656

Days on the Road: 15

Temperature range: 10 to 25 deg C

Diesel: £0.85

TURKEY

Tuesday, 20th May 2008

"Merhaba!"

Well another 20-minute border crossing which is great, overall very organised and friendly, we give 10/10 to Turkey! The roads here are another step up, all motorways and fancy dual carriageways which we are not used to, so we decide to keep driving and try and get to a campsite marked on our map in Istanbul...We had been on the road a long time already, and we eventually arrived in Istanbul around 9 in the evening. Then began the process of finding the campsite which did not seem to be anywhere, and no matter what we did we couldn't find it. So at around 11 o'clock after driving up and down the streets of the decidedly dodgy suburb of Birkakoy, Istanbul, we pulled up on a bit of wasteland behind a derelict fuel station near to what looked like a "homeless glow" and went to sleep in a bit of a grump, and with one eye open...

The following morning we realised that the "homeless glow" was, in fact, a geese coup, and we were sort of by a park by the sea. There were a couple of police cars down the other end, but they just seemed to be hanging out with some other guys having breakfast. We had breakfast ourselves - fried eggs - mmm, cleared up and pulled away, but the police saw us and pulled us over. We anxiously said: "Oh great, what's going to happen now", but when we pulled up to him he said, "Yes yes! You come in I make you Turkish food! Speciality!" We said that was very nice of him, and tried to explain that we were trying to find the camping ground, and he shot off to make some loud phone calls then ushered us around the corner to a guy who was a mobile mechanic and was fixing someone's tyre, but he spoke a bit of English. He said to us, "Istanbul campsite; closed 10 years ago, Atakoy campsite; closed 2 years ago, Birkakoy campsite; closed 5 years ago... but there is one place... they have water.. and parking security...100 meters that way!". Off we trundle, and 100 meters further down the road, we come to a gate through which there was a completely derelict, overgrown and as good as bombed lodge chalet place, with a man who said " yes yes, camping no problem, security no problem" and took us down the lanes of this once-was resort to a place where there were about 4 other motor homes parked on a large flat patch of concrete with vegetation sprouting from every crack.

He showed us the bathroom which was the broken-in door of the nearest chalet which had a...toilet...and a sink with a plastic bowl that you had to fill up to flush the loo as the flush didn't work. "Well we've found the campsite," we said, and realised that at this point we were literally over one wall from the place where we had kipped the night before!!

So we hand washed some clothes and got them up on a line, then headed into town with a chatty taxi driver in a battered old Dacia. We've been excitedly noticing the "old banger of choice" in each country we have been through. Simon thinks that you would all be interested to know that in Czech Rep and Slovakia it's the Skoda 130, in Poland it's the Fiat 500, in Ukraine and Moldova it's the Lada, and in Romania and Bulgaria it's the Dacia 1310. I wish I'd managed to get photos of the 'pimped' up versions of these classics! They'd put any 'Max Power' photoshoot to shame!

Now Istanbul is a city of 20 million, it is huge and pretty mind-blowing. The history is incredible as the city has been the capital of the eastern Roman Empire, and the Ottoman Empire, and was one of the most glorious cities in the world between around 500-1500AD. Many of the old buildings from this era remain, and we saw the immense Topkapi Palace and its luxurious Harem, which along with its grounds take up a very large proportion of the central area of Istanbul. We saw the Blue Mosque, which makes you dizzy looking up at the ceiling due to the size of the space, and detail of the tiling. We didn't bother going to

see Aya Sofya which was a church built in
537AD, then converted into a mosque in the
15th Century, then made a museum in the
1930s. It is meant to be one of the world's
most glorious buildings. I think we were a
bit 'glorioused' out by that point!

We had overpriced kebaps for lunch and
went for a walk which found us in the Grand
Bazaar which is like a mini-city in itself.
It's all inside an old building but has countless narrow streets, containing some 4000
shops. You can get amazing (very expensive) rugs, jewellery, clothes, well everything really, and you just have fun haggling
your way through it. Rhona learnt the word
for "how much" in Turkish, but didn't realise that saying it would invoke a response in
Turkish, which we, of course, didn't understand so had to ask again in English! That's
the point when they probably double the
price!

We decided to walk back to our campsite
from town as it was all along the seafront
through parks and promenades and looked

quite pleasant. Quite a big thing in parks here is to have an outdoor gym, which is where you expect to see swings and round-abouts; you would get all these exercise machines, so you could watch what seemed to be mostly ladies in burkas doing all sorts of squats and thrusts! We thought it was amazing that the machines weren't vandal-ised as they would be in Britain. Another big thing here is fishing, and fishermen line the coast casting their rods. Another very big thing, is Istanbul itself, and it took us 2 1/2 hours to walk home, so another late night for us.

The next morning we were very late heading off towards the east of Turkey. We caught up with our blog entries, sorted some things out around the van and were hung out with a lovely German family of travellers who were also using the 'park-ing site'. We had problems with the water supply. Big problems, which meant that the toilets which were pretty bad anyway were filling up with all sorts of nasties! We also

had a very full porta-loo to empty somehow and with no running water, that was
starting to look too bad to be true! - However, a few hours later some workers managed to resume the water supply, which
helped a little bit but still pretty dire I
would say! But that said we headed off happily at about midday, hoping to get close to
Ankara that evening. We arrived at a place
called Kizilcahamam, which was marked
on the map as a "Thermal Resort" and a
"place of special tourist interest", which we
thought would be an ideal place to spend
a night. There was also a campsite marked
there. We thought it might be some kind
of hot springs or something - cool. Alas, it
was beginning to become apparent that our
days of campsites with all the utilities we
needed were probably over! After searching once again for the campsite marked on
our map, we again ended up wild camping!
So again no shower; we were very smelly
but in a beautiful spot high up in the Turkish hills. Rhona was hoping that her hair

would start cleaning itself as is meant to happen ..hmm... Perhaps a nice cheap hotel would have to be the next stop!

A nice hotel was the next stop in the city of Sivas after another long drive the next day! We watched the scenery change count-less times, from the beautiful forested hilly terrain to the more barren and rocky, red soil/dust to white snow! Turkey is amaz-ingly vast with long distances between large busy cities. Outside the cities, the roads (a lot of which are dual carriageway) that we have been travelling on, have been almost deserted.

The 'cheap hotel' part of the plan once again didn't quite work out. It wasn't in-credibly expensive but was about £30 ra-ther than the £10 which we were hoping for and fitted in with our budget! We keep reading about cheap hotels but never seem to be able to find them. Never mind it was extremely nice and we and all our clothes ended up squeaky clean. We tried out the Turkish cuisine again which is extremely bread-based but very tasty. For lunch, it was a 'Simit' which is a ring of quite heavy bread covered in sesame seeds..lovely.. and then, of course, kebaps for dinner...yummy!

The further you drive east in Turkey, the scenery becomes more and more dramatic, and as we continued past Sivas, the mountains all around were beginning to be snow-capped, then just white with jagged rocky outcrops. The gorges became deeper, the cliff faces sheerer, and the rivers more turbulent. The van had to cope with a lot of strenuous driving, as we climbed mountain pass after mountain pass before twisting back down to the valleys on the other side. At the tops of the passes at around 2200 meters, the temperature would drop as low as 4 deg, and in the valleys (no lower than 1600m) it was never more than 15 deg. The scenery has been so stunning, and we know that our little camera just isn't up to representing the sheer vastness and beauty of what we have seen. Still, I think that those images will be with us forever. I don't know if it was the constant steep hills or some poor quality diesel, but our van seems to be belching out thick black smoke now. Hmm, well all the other vans and lorries do too, so it can't be that bad; maybe we'll blend in a bit more? We got just past Erzurum that night before pulling over. We worked out that we are just about 300 miles from Iraq at this point, but that's ok. There are also quite a lot of army vehicles around which is quite worrying. We're alright here, but a bit further south-east, the empty mountain terrain is used for hideouts by terrorists, so we won't go there!

Turkey has been our favourite country so far, although it seems that each country that we go to is better than the last! It would be great to have a lot more time here, as there are so many interesting things to see and mountains to climb!

Past Erzurum, the scenery continued to astound us to a greater degree than the day before, and as we've just used all our best words on the last paragraph, we don't know how to describe it any more, apart from to just say "WOW"! We have also seen the people get poorer as we've gone east. From the very affluent Istanbul to eastern Turkey where nomadic tribes shepherd their flocks and live in tents. The villages are tiny and remote, normally consisting of a few falling-down stone buildings, and mud out-houses clinging to the mountainside. We have continued to feel welcomed here, and every Turkish person we come across seems to want to speak or just smile to us.

It was only a few hours' drive from Erzurum to Dogubayazit where we made our next stop, so we were there before lunch. It is a frontier town, being a mere 35km from the Iranian border which we plan to go through tomorrow!! Yikes, can't believe we're here already! We found a cheap hotel again, as it would be a good base to do some internet stuff that needs to be done, and sort out all the paperwork for the crossing. Our room has stunning views of Mount Ararat, which is huge, and a great panoramic communal area on the top floor, which makes up for it being very basic and painted luminous green! The streets of the town are narrow and packed with shops, so we decided to go explore. We found a bakery, and bought Peda bread that we just saw come out of the oven for 20p, and tried to eat it for lunch, but couldn't even get halfway through, as it was so big!

There is quite a heavy military presence here, ever since around Erzurum, every village, town, and even remote hotel has a small company of soldiers defending it. In Dogubayazit (or Dog Biscuit as the travellers call it) there are large garrisons with tanks, guns, towers, and lookouts on the hilltops. We are also in the part of Turkey that is inhabited mainly by Kurds rather than Turks. The Kurdish people are a historic people group that has lived in an area that covers eastern Turkey, Northern Syria, western Iran, and northern Iraq for centuries, but their identity has always been denied and repressed by their respective governments, with sharp dealings being dealt to anyone who suggested that they should be recognised as a separate tribe, with separate language and culture.

Anyway, after lunch, we decided to go and visit the Ishak Pasa Palace, which was built between 1685 and 1784 on a crag on a nearby mountain and was very cool. The stone carvings adorning all the doorways, arches, windows and fireplaces were quite something, and its position high up in the crags made it truly spectacular. There was also a mosque that was built before the palace but it had been renovated for use, and looked rather like a small Methodist hall on the inside! Further up the cliff was a proper fort built into the sheer rock face. This was the best bit, as you could climb up to it, and clamber along some exposed ledges to walk along the walls. There are plans to refurbish it, but until then it is quite a ruin, and you can just explore it at your leisure. Rhona had a bit of trouble getting up some of the steeper parts, but luckily there were plenty of young Turkish men available to help her out...

Mileage: 4176 miles

Days on the road: 21

Temperature range: 4 to 29 deg C

Diesel in Turkey is more expensive than in the UK: £1.30/litre!!! No wonder the roads are deserted!

Aya Sofya, Istanbul

Dogubayazit and Mount Ararat in Eastern
Turkey

IRAN

Saturday, 31st May 2008

"Salam aleikom!"

Our last night in Turkey was good, apart from the dodgy kebaps we were served at a nearby eatery. We had to turn down a friendly Kurds offer to go back to his house to drink chai all night so that we could finish off the blog, and make all our arrangements for the next morning when we were to head off towards the Iranian border. Our nights' sleep was slightly disturbed by the whining loud prayer call from the mosque right next door at 3:30 in the morning. They always use the same awful horn speakers turned up full so that they just distort, but I think that is meant to be part of the sound they are going for. It sounds like a wailing Jimmy Hendrix guitar solo sometimes!

We arrived at the border with a little trepidation, to a very long queue of lorries filling up our side of the dual carriageway, but some helpful standers-by directed us to drive up the other side of the dual carriageway right up to the gate where we were ushered to the front of the queue! Another man pulled up beside us and said "I am customs, I get you through very quick, no problem!", and he did, he took us to all the right people to stamp us out of Turkey. You seemed to have to know who the people are, as they were just milling around in plain clothes. He just got them to stamp our papers without looking! We would never have found our way otherwise! We were then ushered through the gate into Iran where all the formalities started again. But once again someone came to our rescue, a very friendly lady this time, and sorted out all our paperwork for us! Amazing, we were through in an hour and a half! It seems in this part of the world, that whenever you don't know where to go or what to do, someone will see you and offer to help, we were trying to find a particular restaurant that evening when someone just overheard us and showed us where it was.

We drove on to Tabriz, which has one of the oldest, biggest (and most interesting) bazaars in Iran, which has 35km of streets all inside a 15th-century building! I don't think we'll make it round the whole thing! We found a guesthouse for £4 a night and put the van in a car park around the back. One great thing we've noticed here is that when you park your car in a car park, you pay an attendant who sits there all night and watches it. In Britain (particularly in Hastings), you pay your parking fee, and the attendants couldn't give a stuff if your car got nicked, they just try to give you a penalty....it seems... The hotel as you can imagine for that price was a bit shabby and noisy but it did the job. We had a great Persian feast in a small restaurant, where we sat on Persian rugs and cushions to eat, it was amazing food and very cheap.

Rhona has now converted to Islam and has to wear headscarves all day, which is not very popular with her. Poor thing is dying of heat and suffocation! Silly rules! Iranian driving is the worst we have yet encountered on this trip, the cities are just a complete free for all, with pedestrians just walking out into the middle of a four-lane street, as that is the only way to cross the road. Iran has the highest road accident casualties in the world, and it is easy to see why, although we both agree that Kenya is probably slightly worse.

We are enjoying the ridiculously cheap diesel here of 1p a litre!! So to fill our tank, and our 3 jerry cans (equivalent to another tank) costs us around £1! Petrol is a bit more, at a pricey 6p a litre. The prices are set by the government, so are the same everywhere. The only problem with this is there is no petrol station (or 5) on every corner as in all the other countries we have visited. Diesel is very hard to get hold of here, we filled up once near the border, but he only allowed us 30 litres due to short supply, and we didn't see another station selling diesel for another 200 miles! Thankfully we got to one just before we ran out!

Tabriz was good fun. A highlight was getting a melon smoothie from one of

the smoothie shops that lined a particular
street. Simon was a bit sceptical seeing all
these pots of freshly made bright green and
orange fruit and veg smoothies, but it was
cold, refreshing, tasty, and hit the spot perfectly. I wonder why they don't have more
of these fantastic joints anywhere else? Another highlight was the bazaar. Our senses
were awakened by all the smells and tastes
of different foods and countless spices.
There were large fruit and vegetable markets with all sorts of fresh produce. There
was every kind of dried fruits and berries,
nuts and seeds that you could imagine. The
biggest difference we noticed between this
one and the one in Istanbul, was the fact
that in Turkey you would have about five
people pulling you from all directions pes-
tering you to buy something from them,
whereas in Iran that was not apparent at
all. People would just politely help you out
if you showed the initial interest. Many
people would chat with us, and invite us
back to their houses for dinner, and we

had some interesting conversations with people. We get the impression that Iran is somewhere that you can't go anywhere fast for talking to people! I think we are spotted a mile off though. That said, it was interesting to hear one person tell us (who will remain nameless in case the Iranian president reads this) how a lot of Iranian people find all the Islamic rules and regulations are choking them, and they feel like they are living in a prison with no freedom.

We had our first proper run-in with the police on our way to the Caspian Sea. It was already starting to get dark and we were planning to pull over to have dinner and camp. This one particular policeman (who may I add was not even in police uniform which made us a bit wary in the first place), was not satisfied with our passport and visa photocopies for his record, because he wanted stamped photocopies; Which of course we did not have! He told us that we had to turn back to the town we'd just come from about 15mins drive back and get copies! Bear in mind that this was about seven-thirty pm and we didn't have a clue where there would be a photo-copier in a large town and all the Farsi language is written in Arabic lettering! But prayer certainly works, and just on the road in we spotted what looked like a computer printer shop and they did photocopies! He didn't even charge us because we were British!

The next morning we drove for about an hour down a very scenic road, only to find it was the wrong one! How annoying!! so we had to turn back and easily found the right one. We visited a village called Masuleh, which is an old village built on a steep mountainside, with the houses all piled on top of each other. The cool thing about it is that the roof of one house is the street of the row above, so you are always walking on someone's muddy roof! These days it looks like its inhabitants live off tourism as it is unbelievably busy with Iranian tourists, and is packed with rows of shops.

We are beginning to feel that we need to

be more careful about where we are sleeping now. This was confirmed when we were moved on by a friendly policeman who advised us that it is unsafe to park where there is no security. So from now on, we will either be sleeping in hotels or hotel car parks in the van, if they let us.

We drove along the coast of the Caspian Sea which is 30m below sea level - the lowest we've been, on the way to the Alborz Mountains just north of Tehran. The fisherman still cast their nets into the sea from the shore like in Biblical times, but we didn't see anyone doing this. We were very surprised that there was a lot of wasteland on the coast with no resorts or even any obvious use. But then women aren't even allowed on the beaches anyway!

Due mostly to the ridiculous price of fuel, the traffic here is horrific, and we are finding the pollution quite difficult to cope with at times, especially on busy roads where there are streams of filthy lorries belching out black smoke. It takes the pleasure out of driving along stunning mountain passes and coastal roads. Being pulled over by the police is also becoming a daily annoyance, they just can't resist it. There never seems to be a large truck to tail at the right moment! Even the ones that don't wave us down, we can see regretting it as we drive past them.

On arrival in the Alborz, we were planning on climbing Mount Damavand, the highest peak in Iran at 5670m. The village where the path starts is called Reyleh, but we again had trouble deciphering all the squiggly Persian signs. We pulled up in a village to ask someone directions, and it turned out we were in the right place and happened to pull up outside the Iran Mountain Federation base camp hostel! Lovely! The deal with the mountain is that you get a Landrover ride up to the 1st hut, and then you hire a mule to carry your bags up to the second hut from where you walk to the summit. We just wanted a map to do it ourselves, but they didn't seem to have heard of maps, we hadn't planned long enough in advance to get one ourselves, and hiring a guide was too expensive, so we decided to just go for a day's walk from the village instead. It is so beautiful here, lots of steep-sided valleys and cliffs.

We took a taxi to the bottom of the mountain and walked up the path where you are meant to have a Land Rover take you up to camp 2, but we were sure our Matatu would have made it! After that, we climbed a bit higher and realised that we probably could have done the mountain on our own, but we didn't have the information we needed. The walk back was a slog, as we walked back along the road that the taxi had taken us up originally. We were so hot and had run out of water. At one point though, a lorry coming the other way slowed down to say hello, and a boy in the front produced a large bottle of cold water and gave it to us! We were truly amazed at the thoughtfulness!

Once we had got back, we decided to

take down the roof box from our van; it held all our trekking and climbing gear, but strangely seemed to draw an awful lot of attention to us. And right enough, since we took it down we have not been pulled over once by the police, and no one notices us until they see that the steering wheel is on the wrong side and that the drivers are very white! We are very sorry to the lovely couple we bought it from, but it is now sitting in a yard in the Mount Damavand shelter 1 hut!

The road to Esfahan, our next stop was a long one, but the roads were good fast motorways. Rather hot though, it got up to 40 degrees, and that's at 1200m altitude! Not looking forward to a day in the Baluchestan desert to get through southern Pakistan! We felt like we were in the Middle East, driving through the endless rolling semi-arid landscape. Just dust, rocks, the odd shrub, and a few jutting mountains all day.

The city streets in Iran really come alive

in the evening, as many people have had their long mid-day siesta, the shops are open till late, and everyone is out and about. It is quite obviously more touristy here in Esfahan, as after not seeing another foreigner for our 6 days in Iran, all of a sudden there are 2 big fancy hotels full of retired Brits! Many Iranians would stop to chat with us, and one newlywed couple Gheisar and Elham took us for a walk and ended up inviting us back to their home. They wanted to hear us play the guitar and sing, so we had brought the guitar along. They lived in a bank, and I don't think they were allowed to have visitors, as they sneaked us in past the security desk and up the stairs! They brought out trays of melons, fruits, tea and sweets, then as the power went out we serenaded them in the pitch dark! All very surreal, but it must have added to the atmosphere as they seemed to be impressed? Again we were touched by the hospitality, and it brought to mind our attitude in Britain when we see foreigners or people who seem lost. We also found out that the public performance of western music or dance is illegal in Iran, in fact when I got the guitar out of the van, Gheisar quickly took it from me and hid it in a big sack so it would not be seen by anyone!

Esfahan is a truly beautiful city, with its lit up, ancient multi-arched bridges crossing the wide slow Zayandeh river, lined with tidy parks, to the hugely magnificent Imam Square (it's the second-largest city square in the world), lined with historic architecture. We once again met up with Gheisar and Elham, and they took us for a tour of the city's most interesting sites. They also insisted on paying for us just to make us feel welcome in their country! It seems to be a very relaxed place and is full of Esfahanis lying on the grass in the square, or sitting under the arches of the bridges on the river, just enjoying the location. We felt quite honoured to be there. We thought that it seemed incredible that among all this dry landscape, there should be such a green city with impressive water fountains on every roundabout, and men with thick hose pipes watering tall trees, plants and grass lining every road. It was great to have the guides again as you get so much more out of a place, and you get a much better taste of the culture first hand.

Onward from Esfahan, and towards the revered city of Shiraz, takes us through more barren landscapes on more fast good roads. At one point, the dust and shrubs that had been the monotonous backdrop that we had got used to, was suddenly broken by the most incredible gorge that looked like a mini lush paradise with thick vegetation, tall trees, and a bright green/ blue river pooling and cascading over rocks. We made good time so decided to go and see the famous Persepolis on the way, before going to Shiraz to find cheap accommodation. As we drove towards it, we noticed a campsite! Shock horror!! Let's stay here! We have not seen a proper campsite since .. hmm .. Czech Republic! There was also a Landrover parked there with a tent, so it must be operational? Firstly we go to see Persepolis, which was built 2500 years ago by Darius I (the Great) as the most fantastic palace and city every built. 220 years later Alexander (the Greater - obviously) defeated them and destroyed the palace. What is left behind is still more complete than any other building anywhere near that old in the world, and is quite mind-blowing. It is the most impressive sight we have seen so far. The complex is so expansive that you can stand in the middle and just see huge statues, pillars, doorways and walls decorated with such detailed and exquisite carvings in every direction, as far as you can see. Every enormous piece of black rock used in any part of the complex is covered in detailed carvings that tell stories, there is not a blank space anywhere, and many of the pillars and statues reach 30 or 40 meters into the sky! Amazing! We checked into the surprisingly nice campsite, and find the owners of the Landrover to be a couple from Kent doing almost the same route as us!

We have been collecting our thoughts about southeastern Iran and Pakistan, and how and if we are to tackle crossing it. We have had varying reports from different people; the south-east of Iran, and particularly Zahedan, near the Pakistan border, is well renowned for its part in the serious drug trade from Afghanistan, and is a place that many Iranians would say was very dangerous and should be avoided, or that great care should be taken; we have also heard about kidnappings and hijackings in the area. Pakistan again brings a surprised and silent response from many people that we have told we are going there. Everything on the FCO website, safe travel website, Pakistan Embassy (?!), and the British Embassy in Iran says simply "Don't go there", so we are a little apprehensive about that. The other side of the coin is that we have met several other travellers who are doing the same route as us through Pakistan to India and have been told that the British Embassy has recorded quite a large volume of travellers currently crossing this area trouble-free. The way to do it would be to cross it (two days of driving), from 'Bam' in the safe part of Iran, spending one night in the Pakistan border police compound, and getting to Quetta in Pakistan the next day. We would also be phoning the British Embassy in Pakistan for advice and to register with them before we go. We are not altogether ready to give up on our goal, and these amazing words below have been quite an encouragement to us:

The Lord is my Shepherd, I have everything I need.
He lets me rest in green meadows; he leads me beside peaceful streams.
He renews my strength. He guides me along right paths, bringing honour to His name.

Even when I walk through the dark valley of death,

I will not be afraid, for you are close beside me,
Your rod and your staff protect and comfort
me.
You prepare a feast for me in the presence of my
enemies.
You welcome me as a guest, anointing my head
with oil. My cup overflows with blessings.
Surely Your goodness and unfailing love will
pursue me all the days of my life,
And I will live in the house of the Lord forever.

PS. Since this writing this, and repeated failed attempts to post it, we have heard from a couple who have just been through Pakistan in the other direction, and have said that it was quite pleasant, with no troubles at all, so the plan is to go for it as above. We could also go in convoy with the other Landrover if we felt that we needed to.

Mileage: 5760

Days on the road: 29

Temperature range: 26 to 40 deg C

Diesel: £0.01 (no joke)

Persepolis, Iran

IRAN–THE DANGEROUS END

Sunday, 8th June 2008

"Salam!"

Well, Shiraz was pretty rubbish. That is to say that through no fault of 'Shiraz', we had a rubbish time in Shiraz. We started by spending over 2 hours in the hospital to get some antibiotics for Rhona, even though she knew exactly what she needed. It was quite an experience just not being able to communicate with anyone, and trying to understand what we needed to do. Luckily, again an English speaking man called Mohamed who was visiting his brother in the hospital came to our help when sorting things out. He then took us out to an amazing ice-cream shop for ice-creams. Yummy, but he was meant to be showing us where the internet cafe was... The only Internet cafe that was open was painfully slow, and wouldn't let us onto our blog which was quite annoying. We did a lot of walking around in 35-degree heat as well, as unlike Esfahan, the trees here are not very big and don't seem to cast much shade anywhere. We needed to get shopping, but were getting quite annoyed with being constantly ripped off, and not having the knowledge, confidence, or Arabic literacy to deal with it. Hot and bothered, we just wanted to drop it all and get back home to the campsite.

There didn't seem to be much going for Shiraz, there is a big fort right in the central square which we didn't have time to look around, but the rest just seemed to be streets packed full of rather camp men's fashion shops.

We decided to stay a third night at the campsite to get our energy back from being pretty much nonstop since we left the UK and to do a few things on the van. We went into the local town - Marv Dasht to try again to post the blog, but being a Friday all the shops and the one internet cafe there were shut for prayers. Never mind, we managed to get some supplies and we will try the blog again in Yazd the next day. The last couple of days have definitely been a bit of a low point, but we are putting that behind us and are looking forward to Yazd and onward. It was nice to meet other 'over-landers', and indeed quite surreal to think of ourselves as part of this elite group of people. It seems that whilst you are in Europe you are classed as campers, but once you've crossed into Iran you officially become an ...'overlander'... which holds way more respect! It is exciting to hear stories from other overlanders, where they have been, and where they are going. We are a bit concerned though because most other people we have met seem to have 4x4 Landrovers, Landcruisers or even more hard-core off-road vehicles. We are quite smug about the amount of extra space we have in our plumbers' van compared to those cramped things though!

Yazd was very nice, but possibly the best bit about it was the hotel whose car park we slept in... Yazd is one of the oldest still inhabited cities in the world, and the 'Silk Road Hotel' is right slap bang in the middle of it. The buildings are all made of sun-dried mud bricks, layered over with more mud, so are surprisingly cool inside. It's amazing to think that all these houses made of mud, among miles of narrow streets are so old! Helped a bit by the lack of rain here we think. The hotel looked like a bit of a wreck from the outside, but through the door and along a passage takes you into the most amazing tiled courtyard with a fountain in the middle, plants, and sitting areas under the shade. Very relaxing. It is a travellers' hang out, and there were overlanders, backpackers, and travellers from many different countries staying there. It seems to be a place where people arrive and then decide to stay for a while, and we can see why. We met more people who have similar positive stories about Pakistan so that was encouraging. The actual car park where we were sleeping in our van was a bit grotty though, hot, dusty, and no breeze. There was a very nice air-conditioned rooftop terrace with internet access though, so we stayed there most of the day.

We mentioned briefly earlier that we thought that the pollution here was bad, but it is quite a serious problem for Iran. No one walks anywhere here; anyone who's anyone has an old motorbike which they ride like lunatics. Because petrol is virtually free, the cost of motoring is the cost of an old bike and that's it. Cars, lorries and motorbikes never get serviced, so the fumes are horrific, and the resulting pollution brings tears to your eyes. The brown cloud of smog with a sign saying 'Tehran' next to it was no joke!

For your comprehension we have compiled a brief list of Iranian driving rules (there aren't many):

1. Drive on the right-hand side.
Exceptions:
·   *Motorbikes - drive on the left-hand side*
·   *Reversing - it's fine to reverse down the*

wrong side of a dual carriageway if you need to.
·   *Convenience - If it will be quicker for you to drive on the left then do so.*

2. Beep your horn continually.
Exceptions: None.

3. Whoever beeps their horn first has right of way. *If both beep at the same time, then whoever has the loudest horn has right of way.*
Exceptions:
·   *Lorries have right of way*
·   *Motorbikes and pedestrians have no rights, just drive as if they aren't there.*

4. A red light warns you that you no longer have a clear junction; *you now have to push your way through cross-traffic just like any usual junction.*

5. Try not to let pedestrians out to cross the road, *they are very slow and hold you up. If one does indicate an intention to cross, accelerate and swing towards them.*

On a side note, but of equal importance, Rhona wants everyone to know that she is too hot.

After Yazd we drove to Kerman and stayed a night there in the car park of a fancy hotel, very pleasant. After Kerman, we drove to Bam which was sadly all but destroyed by a tragic earthquake on Boxing Day 2003, which killed over 31,000 people. We found our way to 'Akbar Tourist Guest House' (with the help of a friendly taxi driver who wouldn't accept payment) and were very warmly welcomed with tea and dates. We may have preferred ice-cold water though as we are down to a mere 1150m altitude and it was 41 degrees outside. The hostel is being rebuilt as it was destroyed in the earthquake, during which 3 of the people who were staying there died, and the temporary rooms are rather basic. We are now in the zone that the foreign office advises against going to, as about 6 months ago a Japanese tourist was kidnapped from his hotel here, (in fact from our hotel as it turns out), and as a result, a lot of tourists have avoided the area. Our friendly host Akbar is very blasé about it though, ironically as he picks up the phone to inform the police that he has some westerners staying with him, and tells us that if we want to go anywhere we have to be escorted by the cops. We did want to go somewhere as it happens, the 'Arg-e Bam', which is an ancient citadel made entirely out of mud. So once again Akbar got onto the phone to the police, and moments later, a battered old police car turned up with no less than 3 officers armed with machine guns! We squeezed in the back, barrels up our noses, at which point Rhona said, "Ooo, I've never been in a police car before, how exciting!", and they drove us to the citadel, walked around it with us, then gave us a quick drive around it before taking us home again! It was rather strange having armed shadows, but we imagined no one would bother trying to kidnap us!

The citadel was quite something, a sight rivalling Persepolis! We were very glad that we came out here. It dates back a couple of thousand years but was also sadly flattened by the earthquake. What is left is still a vast complex city with cobbled streets, huge mud-brick walls, intricate houses with domed roofs and arched doorways. There is a fairy-tale castle in the middle on a jutting bastion of rock which is very dramatic. It has large gatehouses, towers, and steps, passages and rooms running up the rock to the top remaining. Around the citadel, there are large piles of debris from when walls, houses and archways collapsed, which gives it a bit of an untouched feel, (added to by the fact that we (and our bodyguards) were the only people there). A long drawn out restoration is in progress which could take quite a while. We thought that it was quite an amazing sight as it was, and probably one of the most impressive ruins we have ever seen, but we have seen pictures of it before the earthquake looking so complete, as though it was just built yesterday, it must have been one of the most incredible sights in the world! What a tragedy to have lasted so long and then to be destroyed so quickly.

The following day was a day of utter frustration. We had to have a compulsory police escort to the Pakistan border (about 300 miles), but what that entailed was a police car would lead us to the end of the road then stop us and call for another car to take us a bit further. This process happened 12 times, so there was quite a lot of waiting. Once we were out of the city of Bam, we were straight into the Dasht-e Lut Desert, which at 10 am was 43 degrees C, and the police cars had morphed into camouflage Toyota pickups with masked gunmen in the back. We wondered if we would be able to tell the difference between our army escort and the Taliban if they started following us... There were some cool dunes though.

We planned to get to the border and cross it that day, spend the night on the Pakistan side of the border, then get up early the next morning to cross the vast Baluchistan desert, arriving in Quetta late that evening.

We knew the border closed at 5, so we gave ourselves plenty of time and left at 7:45 am to hopefully arrive at 2 or 3. Only about 50kms from the border, we were stopped for our last changeover, but this time we were kept waiting for 1 1/2 hours in the middle of the day before we were taken on. At one point during this time, one of our soldiers made the anti-western sentiments of the area quite clear to us by saying, "You British are like American and you get shot around here"! Nice!

We arrived at 4:00 to find that the border was closed because it was a public holiday, and all week the border closes at 3:30 instead of 5 as usual, How annoying! Two bad consequences came out of this, the 1st one was that the border didn't open until 9 the next morning, allow 1 1/2 hours to get through it, then add 1 1/2 hours for entering the Pakistan time zone, and we won't be able to set off until mid-day in Pakistan, which makes it a bit touch and go to get to Quetta by nightfall! The second was that

Rhona had a phone interview for a job in New Zealand at 9:00 that morning, but we decided that we would have to leave before that if we were to give ourselves a chance of getting through the border that day. Of course, we were stopped in the middle of the desert by the police with no signal, and they wouldn't wait around for anything, so we couldn't get the call. We could have just left later and Rhona might have had a job. So very frustrated, we waited in the intense desert heat and camped outside the pass- port control building with the wild dogs! We were joined at one stage by a very large Iranian truck driver who we thought looked like Fred Flintstone; he didn't speak a word of English, but just chatted away to us all evening, which was very pleasant. He just wanted to look after us and kept buying us cold drinks, as he couldn't believe that we didn't have air conditioning in our van. The following day he was to be of enormous assistance to us.

So we leave Iran with mixed feelings, on

the one hand, most of the people seem extremely friendly and welcoming, some are astoundingly generous and gracious, and some of the sights are quite spectacular. On the other hand, it is very hot and bound by strict Islamic law. We saw an official sign by the border saying "We want nothing...except for the enforcement of Islamic law all around the world", and there is a definite heaviness carried by the people because of this. There are also pockets of people that seem to have quite an anti-western mind-set, as one of our police escorts made abundantly clear to us earlier. We have found the food here to be so-so, and are fed up with that...bread! Just get me a bowl of crunchy nut cornflakes with COLD milk!

So tomorrow we are heading into Pakistan and probably the most worrying part of the trip for us. It is also our point of no return, as at any point up until now we could turn tail and head back to the UK, but once we have left Iran we won't be able to get back in, and there is no other way around.

We will have to make it through the Baluchistan desert, and we can't say "I don't like Pakistan, I want to go home" if it gets a bit heavy. We will have to carry on to New Zealand!

Mileage: 6682

Days on the road: 34

Temperature range: 34 to 44 deg C

Diesel: £0.01

Yazd, Iran

PAKISTAN

Tuesday, 10th June 2008

"Asalem Aleicom!"

Thankfully, on the morning of our border crossing (after what was a very hot sticky night in the van!), we were joined by our friend 'Fred Flintstone' again! If it wasn't for him taking us around all the different desks and pushing in for us, we would never have made it through! He was a truly honourable Iranian man. At nine-thirty in the morning, the temperature was already reaching the forties, and once again we were downing the cold water 'Fred' insisted on buying us. About an hour and a half later we left Iran and entered Pakistan, where of course the whole process of customs and passport control began all over again. We planned to reach the city of Quetta (400 miles away) before dark, but by now it was already midday Pakistan time, so we were itching to get going. Customs was hilarious! We were welcomed by a very nice officer with the words "cup of tea and biscuits?".... and then later after we'd been waiting for him to stamp our carnet for about 20mins... "I am not wasting your time..." He reckoned we would get to Quetta by 6 o'clock no problem: "very good roads!!" He then told us all about the Muslim faith, while we drank very sweet tea. So at around one-thirty, we were off into Pakistan and the dreaded Baluchistan desert!

We very quickly found out what "good road" meant in Pakistan!! A good road may have some patches of tarmac, and at least one lane for both directions of traffic! On this particular 'very good road' there were places where large sand drifts had come right across the road burying it entirely, and in one place, it was impassable. Here we had to divert off the road and onto the desert to avoid it. One car had already tried this and was completely stuck in the sand, so we decided to try to avoid the deep looking sandy patches by staying on the rocky looking bits. It was rather like negotiating one of the mazes you get on the back of a cereal packet! In some places, large areas of the road had been washed away, which was rather a shock when we were driving at 60mph, and all of a sudden had just a narrow 'bridge' of tarmac to drive on, with sharp drops on either side! There were also no road signs, and the main road quite often very deceptively turned into what looked like a track disappearing into the hills. The only indication of it being the right way was the amount of traffic using it.

At around midnight, after a long hot day of blistering temperatures up to 47 degrees, no lunch and only having had Angel Delight and banana for breakfast, we arrived on the outskirts of the massive city of Quetta, with no city map, just a road name of the hotel we were aiming for. Oops!!...not ideal. We found ourselves driving around slum areas trying to find something that would give us an indication of where to go! Just as we entered the city there was a burst sewer that had pooled over the entire road, which we had to drive through like some kind of sheep dip! The smells were horrendous, but thanks to God we found the main road into the city centre, and somehow we managed to drive right into the area where the hotel was. A friendly policeman then directed us to it just round the corner - incredible! So since it was 1 am we showered and went to sleep in our van in the hotel car park without any dinner, but we'd made it!

We were advised the next day that we couldn't make it to Multan as planned because the road was not good. Having experienced what a 'very good' road was like, we dreaded to think what a road described as 'not good' would be like! So we had to go to Sukkur, which was to the South rather than the East and was potentially going to mean staying an extra night in Pakistan! The road to Sukkur was not bad, and the scenery was quite stunning driving down beautiful mountain valleys next to bright rivers. A few miles out of Quetta we were stopped at a police checkpoint, and assigned a police escort who was to be with us for the rest of our travels through Pakistan. They said it was their duty to keep us safe! It was much more organised than in Iran; after every few miles, one police car would stop where another was waiting to take us on. The only problem was they went at their own, very slow pace, and wouldn't let us stop for anything...hmmm. Even so, we made it to Sukkur before dark. But...a very big but.. when we got there they didn't stop! They took us around the city and out the other side! We managed to stop them to ask where on earth they were taking us because once again, we hadn't had anything to eat since two slices of toast at breakfast, and we needed to eat and sleep. In very broken English we were told that it was too dangerous for us to stay in the city and we needed to go 20km further to the police station where we could stay the night. That sounded good to us, but three hours later we were still driving in the dark! At each changeover, we would stop them and ask them where we were going, and each time they would say, "No problem, 20 km, just follow us!!" We eventually found out that we were going to a small town called Sadiquabad, a good part of the way to Multan! The reason was that this town is just inside the Punjab province which is meant to be a safer area for westerners than Sindh province. If they had only told us this before it would've saved so much frustration. The problem was they were all so incredibly nice and friendly about everything, but so frustrating. The escort on last shift was a crack team of special service terrorist busting agents called "The Elite Punjab Police". Their logo on the side of a battered Toyota Hilux looked a bit like a teenage boy's doodling during maths class with crossed guns spraying bullets out like a fireworks display!

They took us to "the best" hotel in Sadiquabad, which looked pretty grotty, and the owner was not happy to risk having westerners there, judging by the very long conversation in Urdu between him and our

5 police escorts, after which we were told, "There is no place here!". We spoke to the man who was the boss of our bodyguards and told him that we were happy to sleep in our van in the police station but whatever happened we were very tired and hungry and it was late! So that said they took us to a restaurant where we had a Pakistani feast! It was great. We weren't conspicuous at all with five heavily armed special agents accompanying us around the table! We had a great conversation with them. After dinner, they insisted we look at another "best hotel". Hmm...after seeing it we managed to persuade them that we would like to stay in our van at the police station, as it was "like home!"

We arrived at the local police station, drove into the bolted courtyard, and were welcomed like celebrities by all the bemused police officers there. There happened to be a journalist for a daily Pakistani newspaper there taking notes on petty crimes, who just about wet himself when he saw us coming! He wanted to write an article about us and our journey! We were grilled and had our picture taken, and now probably have a whole article written about us in the Pakistani press! We were gutted we never got a copy of it! Simon, of course, had to play a song on the guitar once that was discovered by a nosy policeman, and we were sure it was enjoyed immensely by the prisoners who appeared at the bars of their cells to listen and look at what the commotion was. Then we went to bed, safe and sound.

Our long tiring day did have advantages in that the next day we managed to make it to Lahore and back on target with our schedule. We managed to lose our police escort though as 60mph was too fast for them and they never found us again! They couldn't have been that worried! Once again we arrived at the city with no clue where to go. We spotted a nice looking hotel on the outskirts, with secure parking and decided to ask if we could park and use their facilities, which they weren't too keen about. We asked how much a room was for a night and they replied "$150..." which is just slightly over our budget (was a nice looking hotel). We started asking about other places when they told us to take a seat whilst they had a little private chat amongst themselves. The boss who was a very young well turned out Pakistani man, returned to us and said ..."Well, I don't know what you think but if you like I will give you a room for the night for $50, because you are English, and you are my honoured guests!!" So hey presto!! We spent the night in a five-star hotel as guests of the owner - amazing!! One comment he made was, "how with such a threat of terrorism can you westerners travel around so openly?" What do you say to that? "Eh... we lost our police!!!"

Lahore is no distance from the Indian border, so the next day we arrived at the border early. Once again we found that music speaks louder than words, and we ended up entertaining the customs officers and workers with guitar and singing before their day started. We were entertained in return by two or three of them who performed some fantastic Pakistani singing with drum accompaniment, and of course a cup of chai! It worked wonders, as the border officers liked us and whizzed our documents through the process early! So onwards into India, and we really can't believe we have got this far already. We are certainly looking forward to slowing down and recovering a bit. Overall we enjoyed our time in Pakistan, even though we didn't get a chance to see much of it. All the people are so friendly and smiley, and despite the police presence, we felt safe and very welcome. The countryside was so beautiful, although we didn't see the best part - the Karakoram Highway. It was also a shame as it is a total Toyota country - about 2 out of 3 cars and vans were Toyotas! There were so many Hiaces like ours, all with different modifications and customisations. We (well Simon) would have loved to have spent a while here just loading the van up with all sorts of useful things. One person explained, after the standard ridicule at our lack of air conditioning, how easy and cheap it was to fit over there, and we were very tempted. Our roof rack has also broken due to too much weight bouncing around in the Baluchistan desert, and we could have got a great one there.

So we think it is one of the countries we would most like to go back to, and maybe when things have settled down a bit we will be able to enjoy it.

Mileage: 7869

Days on the road: 37

Max Temperature: 47 deg C

Diesel: £0.45

Our Special forces escort in Pakistan

ENTERING
INDIA

Friday, 13th June 2008

"Namaste!"

By this stage, we have started to wonder whether we should be trying to get through borders as quickly as possible, or whether the continuous offers of cups of tea, biscuits, soft drinks, cakes, and conversations with the border officials that slow us down are part of the experience that we are meant to be savouring. Of course, the India border was no exception. We always get special treatment as we have to go to different people than everyone else to sort out the vans' paperwork, and often we are the only people in the books that day. So in a way, I don't blame the officials for wanting to make it last as long as possible! Friendly as it was, the fact was that we still had the full day's drive to Delhi to complete, and once again we didn't escape the border until the afternoon.

But excuse us for being just a little bit excited.... we have just driven into India! India!! India!!! In 5 weeks!!!! We really can't believe that we have come all this way in

our van in such a short time, but it feels
like a major goal has been achieved and a
huge landmark on our journey. We have already driven more than half the distance
we have to drive to New Zealand, but we
have 3 times as much time to do the rest,
so we are looking forward to taking things
a bit slower from here on in, and the first
stage of our newfound 'slowness' is a stop in
Delhi with a couple from our home church
in Hastings - Steve and Lori. We hadn't actually met Steve before and had only met Lori
once, but they openly offered their home
up to us, and it felt like we were at home as
it was so relaxing. It was also great to have
air conditioning, and we wondered how we
ever coped without it, as we nearly pass out
whenever we go outside now!

Our arrival in Delhi was predictably late
at night, and just after a curfew after which
lorries are allowed inside the city. That
later explained why we were in a complete stand-still jam with countless trucks
squeezing us in from all sides. Never-the-

less we arrived after having driven over 2000 miles on bad roads in the last 5 days and just flopped. We stayed with Steve and Lori for another 5 days recovering as Rhona had started to feel a little dodgy. It was just what we needed.

So we had some time to stock up, sort some things out with the van, and make some plans. We are going to fly over to Nepal to visit the house of our friends who are living in Hastings but are pastors of a Church in Kathmandu. We decided that we wouldn't go trekking there, as we wanted to, as the monsoon has hit early, and it is not a very ideal time for it. Instead, we are going to head north to Kashmir in the van when we return to Delhi, and go right up into the Himalayas. The mountains provide a barrier and once you've driven over a 5300m altitude pass, the rains don't get any further than that. So we will be escaping the heat and the rain in one fell swoop before driving down to the south of India.

We have also just found out some exciting and very unexpected news this week, and that is that Rhona is pregnant!!! Help!!! So that explains why she has been feeling so rough! She is only about 9 weeks down the line, but we thought that we should let everyone know so that you can pray for us! So no more bungee jumping, climbing or scuba diving for her which I know she is devastated about! We will continue our journey as planned, and it will be a very well-travelled baby!

So until next time, thanks for reading, we hope you are enjoying hearing about our adventures, Ta for now xx

Mileage: 8222

Days on the road: 42

Max Temperature: 42 deg C

Diesel: £0.45

NEPAL

Wednesday, 18th
June 2008

"Namaste!"

The day we arrived in Kathmandu, 5 taxi drivers were killed, and strikes and a critical fuel shortage were causing the whole country to be at a virtual standstill. The security situation outside of the capital was also virtually non-existent, and there was a particular danger to tourists driving on the roads outside the city, as they are likely to be held up by armed people who would rob them or kill them. We suddenly felt quite wise having decided to take the plane from Delhi rather than driving here, and also very glad of our local friends who we were staying with. That said, we had a fantastic time in Nepal, we received unrivalled hospitality from our friends' two sons who live in their family home whilst their parents are away in the UK.

We were shown around everything there is to see in the Kathmandu valley and had beautiful Nepalese food cooked for us continually. Unfortunately Rhona's "pregnancy sick" seems to be heightened at the mere smell (not to mention taste) of spicy food...not too ideal here, oh, and we are spending the next month in India!! Our hosts would keep cooking up an 'alternative' that Rhona would be able to eat, but 'not-spicy' to us means 'only little bit spicy' to them, which means 'quite spicy' to us! So Rhona has been an embarrassing fuss pot lately, but we survived! We found it strange to have someone spend a long time cooking wonderful food for us and then not to eat with us. They would leave us to it then gobble some up later in their room.

Due to the security situation, we were not able to go outside of the Kathmandu valley, and many places were closed due to strikes, so we were restricted to the sights in the city which were very interesting. There is a lot of Hindu and Buddhist architecture which is very intricate and ornate. Quite stunning carved wooden and stone doorways, pillars, cornices and overhangs adorn the old palaces and tem-

ples with monkeys swinging from the ban-
nisters. There are so many temples around
the city, some as small as a telephone box,
and some huge complexes. Invariably they
would contain a scary-looking carved god
that people would go to worship, and the
atmosphere was very dark and heavy inside. We also went to a gallery of old Hindu
art, all of which were again very intricate,
but mostly rather graphic depictions of sex
and violence.

On one of our walks around the city, we
turned up outside the Kings Palace where
there were huge crowds and a very large
military presence. It seemed like a bit of
a demonstration about something, and we
were just starting to think that this was the
kind of situation that all the advice tells
you to avoid, as it can potentially turn violent. We walked away and headed for home.
It turned out that it was the ceremony
when the new government was taking the
King's flag down, and turning his palace into
a national museum. Essentially it was the

king getting booted out of power, and a symbol of the countries new start as a republic. Quite a momentous time and it was apparently on the world news?

Our friends run and pastor a church in Kathmandu which their son is leading in their absence. It was the part of coming to Nepal that we were most looking forward to, and we're very excited to get a chance to go there. It was quite an amazing experience, the church members are from the poorest of the poor in Kathmandu, most of them living in the slum areas, and the rest maybe just surviving in makeshift tents next to the polluted river. The men would often have to work up to 20 hours a day, 7 days a week even just to support this life as the pay is so low. The church building itself was a brick shell with a leaking tarpaulin roof accessed by walking down a muddy overgrown path. Despite this, it was filled with people that were incredibly friendly, gracious, and seemed to be smiling all the time. The whole morning was such a joyful time, with much clapping and singing. The whole service was in Nepalese, but occasionally our host would translate what was going on for our benefit. At one point he invited us up to share something about us and sing a song, but kept on asking us to sing more songs as soon as we had finished one! After they preach every week they have a time when they pray for sick people who need healing. Most of the church seemed to come forward, and most of them were healed! There is a 93-year-old lady in the church who lives in the slums, who when she first came to the church could not walk. Now she seems very spritely for a 93-year-old even by UK standards!

Our host took me (Simon) on the back of his motorbike to visit the slums where some of the members of the church live. He goes at least once a week to chat and pray with them, and he wanted to show me some of the living conditions that people live in. I didn't think it was too bad at first, but I was amazed that every house we went into, the owner would run down to the kiosk and buy us some sodas to welcome us. I thought I would burst if this went on, but luckily it was only the first few houses! The homes varied a lot, but were at best one small room the size of a standard double bedroom, for 5 or 6 people to sleep, cook, eat, wash and in some cases work in. Some were quite clean with stone walls, whilst others were very dark, dirty and smelly, walls made of corrugated iron and cardboard with a mud floor. There is no running water or sanitation so you can imagine the smells. One lady had a skin condition which meant she couldn't go out into the sunlight and was literally a prisoner in her home. It was very interesting to see though and certainly puts things in perspective.

So after a long weekend, we are sad to be leaving Nepal. Half, because we are in Nepal yet aren't able to go to the mountains or go white water rafting or anything! We will have to come back and do it properly next time, although we seem to say that about everywhere we go. We are looking forward to getting back to the comfort of Steve and Lori's in Delhi though, and are keen to get back in the van as it has been nearly 2 weeks since we were last driving it!

Mileage: 8222

Days on the road: 47

Max Temperature: 30 deg C

HIMACHAL PRADESH

Monday, 23rd June 2008

"Namaste"

The road to Manali is one of those roads that seems to get longer the further you drive along it. Maybe we were driving on a conveyor belt going in the opposite direction because after 9 hours of driving we had only done about 260 miles and we had to stop for the night. We were still at low altitude, so still quite uncomfortably hot, and we decided to sulk off into a cheap hotel for some cooler air. We met a lovely Israeli couple (well they said they were friends that were trying to be a couple?) driving about on bikes. Even the next day it was another 5 hours until we arrived in Manali. We had hoped to do it in a day - no chance, the roads were too steep, bendy and bumpy, and far too many disgusting trucks in the way to go much more than around 20 or 30mph all the way. We were looking forward to the cooler climate that the higher altitude was going to bring us, as we were quite fed up with the oppressive heat around Delhi making sleep almost impossible in the van. And yes, Manali was much nicer - even below 20 degrees at one point - bliss!

Finding a camp spot in Manali was another story - it's an ultra-touristic location here, and every bit of developable land has been...well...developed! Hotels everywhere. We eventually found a hotel with a slightly secluded car park, and they confirmed that it was fine for us to park there for the night...until around 7 pm, when they told us that we weren't allowed to park there? Oh well, there was another 'overland vehicle' just down the road who turned out to be Brits! They seemed not to have any problems where they were so we pulled in next door!

I think that we can already write a whole chapter about Indian driving even though we have only been through a tiny proportion of the country, but it is certainly the most aggressively selfish driving we have come across. My favourite is the overtaking technique employed by those huge battered old buses, which is to pull alongside you on a blind bend...and then just move over on top of you when a car comes the other way! A lot of times the only thing to do is to stomp on the anchors, and swerve off the road, as you can tell by the number of dents they have that they wouldn't mind too much either way if you moved or not! The other is when someone just flies up behind you horn blaring as if they expect you to just jump in the ditch to let them past! It's amazing how much pleasure it brings just trying to keep one of these cars behind you for as long as possible - comparable to scratching an itch. One major problem is that on a typical 2-lane-each-way dual carriageway, you have people and cows walking, and bicycles, and rickshaws driving slowly on the left, all the trucks driving unmovingly at 20-30mph on the right (to avoid having to dodge rickshaws, bicycles and people and cows), and everyone else (cars, buses and swarms of motorbikes) just has to flitter in and out between them.

So we met Sam and Becky and 3-year-old Isaac, the Brits who are driving a monster 20-ton ex-army 4x4 truck that had been converted into a serious off-road motor home parked next to us. With the amount of ground clearance, we almost suggested that we parked underneath them! Amazing truck anyway with everything you need to live inside. We were still smug though as they have had so much attention on their travels, from people trying to break in, climb on their roof for a photo, as well as aggressive police hassle. Our van now just looks like a white minibus with some stuff on an aluminium roof rack covered by a blue tarpaulin. Would you believe it almost every other car here is a white bus/minibus/jeep (or 'Sumo' as they call them here) with an aluminium roof rack covered with a blue tarpaulin!!! No one even looks at us until we stop and camp! We were even tempted to get some Indian transport graphics painted on the side to blend in even more!

We spent some time in Manali just acclimatising, and enjoying the beautifully perfect climate. We were also preparing ourselves mentally for the mammoth route to 'Leh' right in the middle of Kashmir, and the other side of the main Himalayan range ahead of us. From Manali, the road climbs up and up to the first of four huge mountain passes: the Rhotung Pass at just under 4000m. From there the road goes down and up many times to 5328 meters above sea level at its highest - that's only about 500m short of the summit of Mount Kilimanjaro and is the second-highest motorable road in the world. The road is not always passable it is only open for a few months every year in midsummer when the snow is manageable and has only just opened up this year. Most people that drive it go in 4x4's, there is no fuel for one 250 mile stretch, the temperature drops significantly below freezing, there are precipitous drops right beside the crumbling road, altitude sickness is a potential problem, and there are very limited medical facilities - we must be mad!! Well, we already knew that.

We are pretty sure it will be possible for us though, and other people seem to think so as well. We will give it a shot and not be precious about it if it's too hard and we have to turn back. We will be spending plenty of time making sure we are well acclimatized, although that should be fine as at no point will we be sleeping above 3600 meters, and just take it easy really so we'll see how it goes.

Tune in next time for more exciting news from the edge!!

Mileage: 8606

Days on the road: 54

Temperature range: 18 to 32 deg C

Fellow 'Overlanders'

MANALI TO LEH

Sunday, 29th June 2008

Our last of three nights in Manali was lovely, we'd had such a relaxing time there and this capped it off. As we mentioned earlier, Rhona has gone off all Indian food in her mistimed 'pregnancy sick', and has been particularly missing a bit of a taste of home. The night before, Sam and Becky had us over for macaroni cheese, yey! But we'd heard about a total British hang-out, and the fanciest restaurant in town, that even had roast lamb with mint sauce on the menu! We decided to treat ourselves; we arrived and it was just spectacular - It looked like the nicest poshest place you could go to in the most beautiful part of Scotland. The specials board was full of classic British favourites like roast lamb and baked trout. We enjoyed it greatly and it was just what we needed, we went back to the van very satisfied! It struck us that we would never be able to go somewhere like that in Britain as it would be far too expensive, which made it all the more enjoyable!

We planned to head north over four enormous Himalayan mountain passes to the town of Leh right in the middle of old Tibet, and only accessible during summer when the passes can be cleared of snow. After that, if the security situation is all clear, we will continue the loop around to Srinagar and Jammu before returning past Delhi. If not we'll go back the way we came!

The next morning we arose at 4 am to

tackle the Rohtang Pass early before the weather came in, but found to our dismay that half of Manali seemed to have had the same idea. The road (bad, narrow, steep and muddy) was completely chocker with Indian tourists in guided tour jeeps (big business in Manali) taking day trips up to the pass to see the snow. They all wanted to drive much faster than us and would come up right behind us blaring their horn as if we should just drive off the edge to get out of their way! It was a shame because the scenery was so beautiful. After just 1/2 an hour driving we were in a traffic jam - complete standstill for 1 1/2 hours! The cause seemed to be a patch of slippery steep mud that people kept getting stuck on. Don't know what the problem was though, we had no problems driving over it.

The drops would be severe on the one side with no barrier or anything, and on the other side would often be a sheer cliff of rock overhanging the road. A lot of the way it was just one lane, which made passing a

truck coming the other way quite interesting! How close to the edge do you go? Another 2 hours and we were at the top, which
was a hilarious tourist camp! There was a
small patch of dirty old snow with about
1000 Indians running in it, kissing it, making snowmen in it, and having Yak rides
across it? It was quite funny because they
were all in massive thermal arctic survival
suits which they had been sold on the way
up, but it was about 18 degrees! We jumped
out in t-shirts and found it quite pleasant!

We quickly moved on down the other
side of the pass, and the change was instant-
aneous; instantly almost devoid of all vehicles, the clouds, humidity and day-trip-
pers vanished, and we were surrounded by
big lonely mountains, and blue skies. Aver-
aging 10mph, down an incredibly steep
slope with countless switchbacks, we arrived in Keylong, our destination for that
day. We filled up at a fuel station that had
a sign saying 'next fuel - 365km', and we
found that despite being 3300 meters high,

it felt ridiculously hot. It may be raging monsoon on the other side of the pass, but on this side, it is as dry as a bone, with a very strong sun. We soon realised how easy it is to get sunburnt at this altitude when we went for a walk the next day and were slapping on sun cream every 1/2 hour.

Rhona has still been struggling with feeling sick every day, and we were beginning to wonder if all this was a good idea. Maybe we should just pack it in if we're not having a chance to enjoy it properly. The walk we went for was meant to be a short two-hour trek up to a Buddist monastery on the hillside, but after 4 hours we had still not made it due to tiredness, so we just went back. It is a real shame as two things that Rhona loves is Indian food, and walking, and she's unable to do either. Well, the altitude seems ok so far, so we'll continue slowly up the valley and stop another night before going for the big passes which is going to be so cool!! As long as Rhona can enjoy the views, and Simon can enjoy the driving we're ok!

When we headed off up the valley, the road seemed better than what we had been on so far, and we reached our designated camp spot, the village of Darcha - the last permanent settlement for the next 200 miles by 11 am. We (well Simon coz Rhona can't stomach it) got a big slap-up Indian lunch from one of the many tent 'dhabas', which cook up cheap nosh for truckers and travellers, then we got a cup of chai...after that, we realised that there was nothing else to do there so we said: "sod it, let's just go over the first pass and sleep on the other side!". So we did! This pass takes you up to just under 5000m which is very high, and we were glad of our 5 days acclimatising in Manali and Keylong. At about 4500m there was a tiny remote mountain lake with a man with a single pedal boat thing for hire which we thought was quite hilarious, and were very tempted to go on it just because of the bizarreness of it! It was like the ones shaped like a duck that you get in the boating lake in Alexandra Park in Hastings!

Continuing onwards, the road would be horrendous one moment allowing us to only crawl along at around 5mph, and then there would be an amazing, new tarmac road for a while. There seemed to be teams of men and women along the road just continually fixing it. They would stir their huge pots of tar over great black fires and chip away at rocks to fill the holes.

At one point one of the many rickety river bridges that consist of a couple of steel girders with sheets of steel or wood laid across them had collapsed. They are quite hair-raising at the best of times, and the noise driving across them as the unfixed steel plates clatter and move about is quite indescribable. At some points, the sheets would have shifted revealing large gaps that had to be driven over. Well with this particular one, the only option was to drive through the deep cascading river at a 'fording' point next to it. We had done similar before, but this river looked very deep and very fast compared to any of the other ones.

We concluded that other vehicles (albeit mostly 4x4's or trucks) had made it, so we would be able to. I (Simon) knew the engine air intake should be ok as that is halfway up the side of the van by the driver's door, but I was a little concerned about the exhaust going too deep underwater and choking the engine. That would be awkward - stuck in the middle of a raging torrent with a flooded engine...hmmm... Well, there was nothing for it but to take the plunge, and after a bit of encouraging advice from a motorcyclist (who incidentally, being on a motorbike was able to ride straight over the bridge) we did. I just kept it in first and kept the revs and speed up and hoped for the best. The first section was OK at around 50cm deep, but then we just dropped down a big step and water started pouring over the front of the van up to the windscreen! I knew that the exhaust pipe would be underwater, so I floored it and hoped that the pressure of the gases would overcome the weight of the water. The rear wheels

bounced and scrambled over the slippery
rocks on the river bed and then all of a sudden we were on the other side! Yey! What
fun! I was overwhelmed by an overriding
desire to do it again! Luckily Rhona managed to talk some sense into me and we
drove on!

Up to the top, we were realising just how
much the altitude sapped power from the
van. It was pathetic; we rarely got out of
second gear even on fairly level ground!
Over the top we were presented with the
biggest landscapes we had ever seen, mountains and glaciers close up on both sides,
then opening up into a vast wide valley
below. The bottom of the valley looked flat
and green but was scarred top to bottom by
a spectacularly deep canyon. It was quite
amazing. We arrived at 'Sarchu' which is a
kind of tented sleepover point for truckers,
and some travel companies have their
camps there as well. The camp is at a low
point on the road before it begins to climb
up to the next big passes (two more to go).

That said it was still up at around 4500
meters! We drove off the trail and found a
very secluded camping spot by the canyon
with beautiful views. Rhona had her afternoon snooze, and then we were moved on
by some people who told us that we were
destroying nature by sleeping there. So we
drove back up to the littered dust bowl of
Sarchu and parked up with the truckers.

By 10 pm the area was completely awash
with trucks stopping for the night, so we
decided to get up at 4 am again to try and
beat the rush. We couldn't imagine anything much worse than being stuck behind
lines of lorries belching their way up the
single lane passes. Our plan worked and we
were on the road before 5 just as the sun
was rising and the truckers were emerging
from their slumber. We had a clear road
to ourselves and didn't see another vehicle
for around 2 hours which was lovely. We
climbed up to the next pass - 'Lachlung La'
which was higher than the last, drove down
through more incredible scenery which had

become very desert-like, and up to the
highest pass - the Tanglang La, which at
5328m/17500ft is the 2nd highest motorable road in the world. Incidentally, the
highest motorable road in the world at
5601m is the 'Khardung La' just around the
corner, and we were quite tempted to drive
up it just to say we had done it, but it turns
out you need all sorts of 'inner line per-
mits' for going close to the disputed borders with China and Pakistan? So we chose
to be satisfied with just the 2nd highest! At
one point the road just diverted off into a
massive dust flat where we had to pick our
route across this huge bowl at the bottom
of the valley to the other side. The problem
was that this dust was like talcum powder
up to a few feet deep in places, and it was
a little tricky finding our way through the
more shallow bits to avoid going under! All
said, after 9 bone-shaking hours we arrived
in Leh with plenty of time to settle in! The
underside of our poor Matatu had received
a good battering from rocks, and the engine

seems a bit ratty, but all in one piece!

This little excursion has re-written our preconceived ideas on the word 'remote'... We've realised that when you drive for three days seeing no permanent civilisation, just occasional summer-only tents, housing people to service the road that is only open for a few months a year, it could be classed as remote?

Leh turned out to be a lovely town. The first thing we noticed was that there was no rubbish anywhere unlike the rest of India which is quite frankly a tip. They have a 'no plastics' policy which is quite impressive. It's also in the rain shadow of the Himalayas, so its annual rainfall is on par with the Sahara desert. Saying that it did rain briefly whilst we were there - typical! We found a beautiful guesthouse to stay at though, with stunning views across the valley towards snow-capped Himalayan peaks.

Mileage: 8918

Days on the Road: 58

Temperature range: 3 to 29 deg C

Approaching Tanglangla 5330m above sea level

TRAPPED IN LADAKH!

Monday, 30th June 2008

"Jule!"

E verything seems to be colliding in Kashmir, worlds, religions, land, and people. We seem to have run into a bit of a trouble spot. Just 2 days after we crossed over the Rohtang pass from Manali towards Leh, it was closed down due to some collapse or snowfall or something. That was lucky we thought, but that is more like a bridge burnt as we won't be able to go back that way again. Now that we are in Leh in Ladakh (separate to Kashmir), there are only 2 roads back out of it. The first is 3 days south over the mountain passes the way we came towards Manali, which is closed off, the other is 4 days west to Srinagar and Jammu inside Kashmir, which is what we had planned to do. Kashmir is safer now than it has been for years, and there have been very few disturbances for quite a while, but we just found out that the very day we crossed the Rohtang pass, unbeknownst to us, violent protests involving killings began in Srinagar and are still going on now. Travellers are not going through there, and the advice is that we don't either. So as you can see we are in a bit of a predicament. Either we wait for the Rohtang pass to open again, or we wait for the situation in Srinagar to settle down. There is an airport here, but unfortunately, we have the van to think about.

I'll give you a brief history of why there are so many problems in Kashmir. It all goes back to the British - it had to really... Around 1600AD, the Brits arrived in India, and by 1858 they had formal control over an area extending to current-day India, Pakistan and Bangladesh. When Independence from the Brits came in 1947, the Muslims, Sikhs and Hindus all wanted their separate states. The problem was that there were no clearly defined Muslim or Hindu areas, and when they drew the line separating Pakistan (Islamic state) from India (Hindu State), millions of people quickly tried to relocate to their 'side' of the line. The result was mass genocide. Kashmir was

Muslim dominated but had a Hindu maha-
raja, so he, under military pressure decided
to sign his state on as part of India. Pakistan disputed this immediately and within
2 months of independence, they were at
war with each other. Two years later, the
UN stepped in and drew a line down the
middle of Kashmir dividing it between the
two countries as a temporary fix, but it
has remained the same ever since. Neither
country accept the line, they both want
the whole lot, so they keep fighting over
it. Muslim extremists have caused havoc in
the area, committing repeated attacks on
Hindu interests.

The incident this week was because there
is a very holy Hindu site within the Muslim Kashmir, which thousands of Hindus
make a pilgrimage to every year. The Indian
government transferred some surrounding
land to the Hindu pilgrimage organisers
so they could put up some huts and toilets for the pilgrims use. Now the Muslims
feel cheated of land, and it has kicked off

major demonstrations. Everyone in Kashmir hates Indians, and would rather be part of Pakistan, but it's all just religious. Even though the area has been at peace for a while now, tensions run high and it just takes something pathetic to send it loopy. All the same, it is causing us some problems as we have no way out of this valley.

After speaking with various other people, and looking up articles on the web, it seems that even a quick dash through Kashmir to get out of the valley would be out of the question. The police there say that tourists have nothing to fear, as the violence is not directed at them, and they will be perfectly safe as large police forces are guarding the tourist spots and hotels. In contradiction I read one article in a Kashmiri newspaper that said that tourists were leaving in the middle of the night to escape Srinagar, so we thought that it must be pretty bad. Just how bad was realised when someone turned up at our guesthouse in Leh who had just come from Srinagar.

He was there when the trouble started and tried to leave, but the so-called police protection forced him at gunpoint to stay in a particular hotel and pay a lot of money. He managed to break out in the middle of the night to escape over here but it was quite a nasty experience.

There is one other way out, and that is to drive back to just before the Rohtang pass, then take a left. This takes you down another valley on a very long detour of several days back around towards Delhi, but is apparently the worst road in India! Judging on how we managed on the Manali-Leh road, we think it might be pushing it a little!

That said, we are enjoying staying in Leh very much. It has a very pleasant cool climate (jumpers required in the evenings), very interesting streets, shops and sights, and beautiful views.

Some other people have said that they think that the Rohtang pass is open again, but can potentially close at any moment, so I think that our only option is to go all the back the way we came, along the mountain passes back to Manali, and hope that the Rohtang pass is open when we get there. We are not particularly looking forward to it as the high passes are quite strenuous, and the high altitude makes you feel pretty rubbish at the best of times. Still, we will leave tomorrow (Tuesday) and hopefully arrive in Manali late on Thursday. Wish us luck!

We have also been re-thinking our plans to drive down to the southern tip of India and then up to Chennai to ship our van to Australia, as this time of year is monsoon season and is quite unpleasant to be travelling around those parts. Instead, we are thinking of just getting down to Mumbai, and shipping the van directly to New Zealand from there thus 'skipping' Australia! We will still fly to South East Asia, and spend some time in Thailand and Malaysia whilst the van is getting to NZ before joining it there.

Mileage: 8928

Days on the road: 61

Temperature range: 12 to 28 deg C

THE GREAT ESCAPE!

Tuesday, 8th July 2008

When we drove over the mountains the first time, we found that although very beautiful it was quite a tough experience. The roads were bone-shakingly awful, we were struggling to breathe, couldn't sleep, and had constant headaches from the altitude. The dust was so thick in the air that it just infiltrated everything until you could feel it gritting between your teeth, and the isolation of it kept us a bit worried. Long before the end, we were quite keen to be getting off the mountain and into the comfort of civilization, but at an average speed of just 10mph (in some sections we were only able to make around 3mph) the end was a long time coming. So understandably we were a little grumpy about having to do it all again - and we'd already seen it all! But we set off, this time planning on doing it in just two 12 hour days. We kind of got it into our heads that we just had to do it, and strangely came around to the idea more. What we didn't expect was that we would actually find it much more enjoyable the 2nd time, and the 2 days seemed to go by very quickly.

For a start, because we had already done it, and then stayed in Leh for 4 nights at high altitude, we were much better acclimatised than we were the first time around, and even at the top of the highest pass, we didn't feel the effects of the altitude at all. We managed to get a system going to combat the dust, as whenever a truck went past, or the wind blew kicking up a cloud, we would quickly wind the windows up and close off the air vents, before opening them up again when all was clear. That seemed to work well. Unfortunately, the roads hadn't got any better, and not too long after we started up the first pass, we heard a crack from the back of the van, followed by a clattering every time we went over another bump. We found out to our dismay that on one of our rear wheels, 2 of the 3 leaf suspension springs had snapped, leaving it hanging on just one. There was nothing else for it, we just had to nurse it even slower over the remaining distance back to Manali, hoping that the final leaf spring didn't snap as well...

At one point, we came across a couple of motorbikes stopped at the side of the road. We slowed down to make sure they were OK, and it turned out he needed some tools to fix something on his bike. We tried all ours, but they didn't quite fit, so we left them to it. A short while later, having collared someone else to help them, they overtook us, but five minutes after that they were stopped at the side of the road again, this time with a flat tyre! We once again offered our tools, but in trying to fix it he put one of our screwdrivers through his new inner tube! Once again we had to leave them, this time with an army truck that had stopped, but we never saw them again, so hope they are OK?! Talk about having a bad day!

All the way along the road there were groups of workers employed to just live up there all summer and repair the road. It looked like horrible work using the most basic tools to break up rocks and shovel dirt into holes in the road. Every time we passed a group they would try to stop us and we realised that none of them had any water or food for the work they were doing. This was quite a shock and we wish we had brought more food with us to give out. It seems that they survive on donations from truck drivers and other road users.

We had nearly run out of water by the time we reached our mid-way camp! They must work every light hour of the day and probably get paid 30p a day or something.

If anything, the views seemed to be better this time around. Maybe just seeing them from an opposite angle gave a different perspective? The sky was the most amazing deep blue colour we had ever seen, compared to the first time which was rather cloudier. This alone made it quite spectacular. At the high halfway camp at Sarchu, the first time we had felt so rotten and didn't sleep, but this time we felt fine. We almost wanted to stay there for a few days! It was great to feel the cold (down to around 2 degrees), and the stars at night were inexplicably stunning.

When we got back to the Rohtang pass, thankfully it was open, and it sort of felt like a gateway back into India! Ever since crossing it a week before, and moving into Ladakh, everything has felt so different, peaceful and disconnected from the rest of India. This was like a wakeup call, because all of a sudden the crowds were back in full force, and people were trying to sell us everything. When we got back to Manali we were surrounded by all the shoe fixers, masseurs and snake charmers (it's ok, Rhona soon got rid of them), and we just said: "welcome back to India!"

The next day we spent in a garage trying to get our suspension fixed, and we realised the disadvantage of taking an old van. That is that when it breaks, it is near impossible to take anything apart as it is all rusted and fused together. In the case of our van, 12 years sitting on muddy building sites in GB hasn't done it any favours, and it took 5 people 5 hours to get the old suspension off! In the end, they had to cut the last bolt with a welding torch! They, of course, didn't have the right replacements, so we got a bit of a customised mish-mash of different suspension springs that went together to make it about the right strength, but now one side of the van is higher than the other. Never mind, after waiting 8 hours for this one, we weren't particularly inclined to insist that they take the other side off and do that as well!

The garage was in fact just a dusty patch of oil-soaked ground, swarming with flies by the road with a tin hut next to it. As we were there all day, we got our usual attention from the many Indian tourists who wanted to see the van and take our pictures. Some of them were very pleasant. One man (a local taxi driver) insisted on buying us tea and crisps for our wait which was very kind. He took us to the cafe down the road, but when Rhona asked where the toilet was, he took her behind his car parked on the main road, and said "there!", "We are very open in India!" Rhona wasn't convinced, and made him take her to a 'proper' toilet which we had to pay 3 rupees (4p) for!

So the next morning we planned on leaving Manali to go to Shimla which is another hill station town at around the same altitude on the way back to Delhi. Hopefully, we will be able to stay there for a while relaxing and sorting out things for the shipping of the van to New Zealand and hopefully onward visas etc. Simon finds out if he will get on his flying course this week as well, so we are very anticipant of that. Rhona's nursing registration is still not sorted out, and she is still wondering what she will end up doing in NZ now that she is not quite as 'employable' as before!

Mileage: 9237

Days on the road: 64

Temperature range: 2 to 26 deg C

THE SCOTTISH HIGHLANDS TO THE TAJ MAHAL

Friday, 11th July 2008

Walking along the high street of Shimla was like walking along the high street of any historic town in Britain. It was built by the Brits and became the summer capital of all of India when all the Viceregals and officials came up here to escape the oppressive heat of the plains in Delhi. It is literally perched on the top of a very steep narrow ridge up at 2200 meters in the Himalayan foothills. The views either side would have been amazing if not for the fact that it was pretty much foggy the whole time we were there. The buildings were all very typical stone-built Victorian architecture with bay windows, slated roofs and all. We could so easily have been in England - the weather, temperature, and there were even lots of Indians walking around! The only difference was that being in India and surrounded by forest, there were heaps of Monkeys everywhere.

The problem we had was that being on such a steep slope, there was nowhere flat to park the van and camp, and the hotels were all comparatively expensive. We found a half-decent one and stayed there for three nights before deciding we couldn't afford to stay any longer and moved on. We walked up to the highest point in Shimla which is through the forest up a very steep hill to a Hindu temple, dedicated to Hanuman - the monkey god. Coincidentally there are indeed lots of monkeys all over it, although we think that is possibly more down to the habitat than spiritual connection. It was very cool to see the monkeys climbing and swinging on everything so close up though, and the babies were so cute! This was far more interesting than the temple itself!

After that, whilst Rhona took her pregnancy-induced daily nap, Simon went to see the 'Viceregals lodge' which is where the rulers of British India lived at the full extent of their power and held meetings whilst they were there. Kind of like the 10 Downing Street equivalent. It just looked like a really grand Scottish castle which

was quite amazing. It was completely untouched and unrepaired, with all the original cast iron exterior staircases that
looked less than safe, and huge gardens
that they couldn't keep up with. Overall
it was much more original and complete
than anything you might see in Scotland. It
looked like the ideal place to have a posh
cup of coffee and a piece of shortbread in.
Unfortunately, it is in India and they have
converted it into an advanced study college, and so now it actually gives off a bit
of a Cambridge University college feel. A
group of us were given a tour of the inside where we saw the rooms where famous
meetings with Gandhi had taken place, and
the table they used to redraw the borders of
India at independence. A very big chunk of
Indian history really.

That evening we decided to treat ourselves and went to the poshest hotel in
Shimla - the Oberoi Cecil for dinner. It was
very posh! It would be the equivalent to one
of the fanciest places in London, tailed but-

lers and all, with rooms costing hundreds of pounds. We weren't quite sure what we were celebrating, but we decided that it was for our new future family member! The next day Simon found out that he got on his pilot course in NZ so it could be for that as well. We just thought that if we can't do this sort of thing in India, then when will we be able to do it? To put it into perspective, with starters, bread, mains, wine and everything it came to around £30 - about the same as a normal meal in the UK! Not bad! We'll go back to dhal and rice tomorrow!

After Shimla, we waved goodbye to the beautiful cool mountain air that we had enjoyed for the last two weeks, and set off on the huge 12-hour drive down to Agra, one of the hottest parts of India - in the middle of summer! Luckily (or unluckily - we're not sure yet) since the monsoon has come in the temperatures have dropped a little, so instead of 50 degrees, it's only around 35, but the humidity is something else. Even at night time you are just constantly sticky with sweat - it's disgusting!

We arrived in Agra at around 8 pm and found a guide-recommended place that had a large enough parking area for us to camp in, but it turned out to be a mosquito-infested patch of boggy mud. We went to the reception and they wanted 600 rupees a night to camp there!! (We normally only pay 50-100 rupees) It was quite annoying that they wanted to take advantage of us. They wouldn't budge on the price, and due to the late hour, we had no choice but to stay there. Later we found a decent hotel nearby with an air cooler for just 400 rupees a night! It's funny how you get normalised to the price of certain things in an area because although it wasn't a lot of money by British standards, it was a small fortune by Indian standards!

Anyway, we headed off for our tour of Agra's sights with our cycle-rickshaw man who had attached himself to us. 1st stop - Taj Mahal which was jaw-droppingly spectacular, and so much more impressive in reality than in photos. It was worth getting a local guide who showed us how the floral designs that covered the entire building were all intricately made up of tiny pieces of semi-precious stones all from many different countries. Inside the mausoleum, even though you are not allowed flashes or lights, he took in a torch, and showed us how as you move it over a flower design, each gemstone would light up and glow individually - it was so beautiful. Amazing to think that it was all just for one person's tomb! It was built by Mughal Emperor Shah Jahan, for his wife Mumtaz Mahal who died giving birth to their 14th child in 1631! Supposedly Shah Jahan wanted to build a mirror image Taj on the other side of the river in black marble (way more expensive than white) for himself, but his son Aurangzeb overthrew him and imprisoned him in Agra fort for spending all the kingdoms money!!

We went on to see said Agra fort next, 2 km up the river, which has good views of the Taj. The classic thing to do is to get a picture of you on the rampart with the Taj Mahal in the palm of your out held hand - so we did that... It was getting a bit hot at this point, so we turned down our rickshaw drivers offer to take us to all the other sights in Agra and went back to the hotel.

We have been quite surprised by the quality of the roads outside of town, in that they are actually quite good. There has just been an explosion of national highway building in India lately, and if any of them are not dual carriageway, then they are being made so. The problem is that Indians don't seem to understand the concept of dual carriageway being that one side is for one direction, and the other side is for the other direction. They (mainly motorbikes and rickshaws, but also cars, buses and lorries) just use each side as a separate road. Normally you can see them coming, but at one point Simon was driving, and we had been trying to get past a lorry for ages. Eventually, he pulled over and we began overtaking. At this point

Rhona started freaking out, Simon looked at her, then at the lorry, then questioningly back at Rhona who was by this point practically sitting on the headrest covering her face! He then looked forward, and there was a rickshaw driving up the wrong side of the road straight for us! We weren't going too fast and he had stopped by this point so we were ok, but it definitely keeps you on your toes!

So that was on the way from Agra to Jaipur - our next stop in Rajasthan where we are now. We have passed a major landmark on our trip, and have driven over 10,000 miles since we left Hastings which is pretty cool.

Mileage: 10,005

Days on the road: 71

Max Temperature: 35 deg C

In The Red Fort, Agra

RAJASTHAN

Friday, 18th July 2008

Jaipur was a city of luxury for us, we stayed in an amazing hotel (compared to most of the other hotels we have stayed at), with air conditioning, marble floors and everything! The city is also quite historic and is surrounded by hills all with ancient forts and temples on them overlooking the city. The old city walls have always traditionally been painted pink, and so Jaipur has been dubbed 'The Pink City' and glows when the sun goes down. They have been renovating all the pink walls, and old buildings, fixing them and making them more pink, and we thought that it was all starting to look a bit tacky. We stayed for just three nights before re-thinking our budget and getting bored. We had a day of sightseeing where we went to see the old city palace which was rather dull, another viewing tower for the ladies of the palace which was just completely covered in scaffolding and builders rubbish but was quite cool none-the-less. It had some tiny passages, staircases and cubbyholes with tiny wooden shuttered windows that the ladies could watch the processions below from without drawing attention to themselves.

Lastly, we saw an ancient astrology and astronomy site. It was basically full of enormous sun and moonlight measuring equipment, including the largest sundial in the world (27 meters high!), all built out of stone and marble. The instruments were built near the beginning of the 18th century and still work perfectly today. The large sundial measures time accurate to 2 seconds!! Unfortunately, the day that we went it was pouring with rain and none of it was working at all! It was very interesting though, and quite a bit different to all the normal palaces, forts and temples that we have become quite accustomed to. A highlight was walking to the top of the big sundial, and getting the view of the old city and looking down on all the different instruments scattered around the area.

Walking around town that day was quite interesting as the heavy rains combined with poor drainage caused many of the streets to be flooded. Wading through them is a bit of an unknown quantity - you don't know what you are walking through! - Yuk!

We found ourselves getting quite irritated by all the hecklers around here, you can't walk for 1 minute without about 5 rickshaw drivers telling you where you should be going, and how cheaply they will take you there. You can also almost guarantee that anyone coming up to you to talk, no matter how honest they seem is going to try to extort money out of you. One time a friendly man came up to us and said, "Can I just ask you something? Why do western tourists not like to talk to Indians?", "we do" we replied, "It's just a bit irritating when they're just after our money." "No, no, no," he said, "I just like to talk and make friends... anyway would you like to see my shop?"! Another time, someone caught us coming out of a restaurant, and started a very friendly conversation with us, piling 'gifts' of beautiful handmade puppets on us. We said we couldn't give him anything for them but he said "money is not important, I want you to have these things", he wouldn't take them back, but when we said we had to go he said, "So what can you give me?" When he realised we weren't going to give him anything, he took all his things back and cleared off! This has become quite typical of very many of our experiences in India.

On our first night in Jaipur, we found a rooftop restaurant (most of the restaurants around here seem to be rooftop) just around the corner from our hotel that was just fab, we pretty much decided to go there every night! All the tables and chairs were individually designed wrought iron in a kind of modern art style which was quite cool. We could have just spent all our time between our hotel and this place! Sadly, a lot of our time was spent trying to sort out our New Zealand visas and the shipping of the van from Mumbai, now that it is all a bit more difficult than before. It is possible though and it will be done!

We are just realising how excited we are at the thought that we are going to New Zealand and that Simon is doing his flying course. He has had 'I believe I can fly' stuck in his head ever since finding out, and keeps driving down the dotted line in the middle of the road as though it was a runway!

Our Next stop is Udaipur, about 400 kilometres south of Jaipur, but we are in a bit of a dilemma. Basically, we are trying to sort out the shipping of the van to New Zealand, but the shipping agent can't do that unless we have our flight tickets to Auckland to prove that we will be there to pick it up; We can't book our flights until we have our NZ visas; we can't get our visas until we have a receipt that the flying course fees have been paid; we can't pay the fees until our bank gets its act together, and we are waiting to hear from them. To add to that, we don't know if we will even be able to arrange our visas in Mumbai, or if we have to go all the way back to Delhi to do it. Oh well, we just decided that we have to keep moving in the general direction of Mumbai, and if one or both of us has to go back up to Delhi then so be it.

Udaipur then is a very beautiful city - they call it 'the Venice of the East', due to its position on a lake with a grand brilliant white palace out in the middle of it. It gives a very fantastical and romantic feel. Unfortunately at this time of year the lake is mostly dried up, and it is not until the end of the monsoon that it starts to get full (before promptly drying up again!), so it is not quite as beautiful as it could be. The locals are very proud that large portions of the James Bond film 'Octopussy' was filmed here, and most of the guesthouses show it in their restaurants every evening, and have done so since nineteen seventy whatever when it came out by the looks of things! We watched it the first evening we arrived on our guesthouse rooftop terrace, and we must say it was extremely cool to watch a fairly well known iconic film, during which we would look to the left and say "Ooo, that's over there", then to the right, "that was down there!"

Our guesthouse is very handy being only

about £2.40 a night. Our room kind of reminded us of the servant's quarters that
people in Kenya had, but that's fine, it's
very pleasant, clean, quiet, quite pretty,
and does good food. We found out that we
can submit our visa applications in Mumbai, which is good news, but we may as well
spend as much time as we can here sorting
things out rather than in Mumbai which is
the most expensive place in India to stay by
about double the nearest competitor.

Now that we are eating out every day,
we are discovering that almost any restaurant we go to is basically a carbon copy of
all the others. They all just do Indian food,
and then all kinds of Italian, Chinese, Israeli
and continental food with a strong Indian
twist. We just resigned to the fact that once
you have found a decent place, you're just as
well going there every night! It is rather tiring though having no variety what-so-ever.

We did the tour of Udaipur with its impressive stone carved temples, and city palace overlooking the lake. All very grand and

ornate, in fact, the whole city is really beautiful and much quieter than any of the other
cities in India. We think it is definitely the
nicest in India so far, and one of the best cities on our trip. We also got an elephant ride
here which Rhona has been going on about
ever since we arrived in India, so that was
good and a lot of fun. When we were lum-
bering down the street, our elephant would
keep getting distracted by things, like fruit
stands where it would try and pinch some
snacks! The stall keepers didn't seem to
mind though, and they would give it man-
goes which kept it happy!

We spent four nights in Udaipur overall as
it was so relaxing, and have been trying to
make the transition from living in the van
to living out of a rucksack in preparation
for the month of backpacking through
South East Asia before going to New Zealand. It felt weird to be packing the van
away so soon, almost like it was signalling
the end of an era. Well we have to move on
and it's the only way forward, so we'll just

look forward to what will happen next!

We headed off from peaceful Udaipur in the direction of Mumbai - the big city of India, splitting the journey at a city called Baroda. Once again the state of the road was a pleasant surprise. It was a beautiful tarmac motorway most of the way, lined with stonework and marble stalls. We are very tempted to buy a slab of marble while we're here to make a coffee table out of as it's so readily available and probably very cheap. Baroda, however, was not so pleasant! Described as a cultured, harmonious university town, it, in fact, seems to be a pretty dirty, smelly and unfriendly place. We didn't seem to be able to get away from the beggars and children constantly tugging and pulling at us to get some money. It was so hard because we felt so sorry for them but also powerless to help – it's hard to explain.

We had a bit of a hunt for a reasonable clean hotel, which was also difficult to come by. We ended up in the aptly named Swastik Hotel with Nazi symbols everywhere! We were greeted by stares, not smiles in contrast to our general experience of India so far, and very brash, un-trusting hotel staff. We decided to stay for only one night, but when we discovered wireless internet in our room we got so excited. With so much that we needed to do online, we decided to stay two nights spending all day on the web venturing out only to eat!! Brilliant!

Mileage: 10,477

Days on the road: 79

Temperature range: 30 to 35 deg C

A temple in Udaipur

BOMBAY
(MUMBAI)

Sunday, 27th July 2008

Our drive to Mumbai was to be the final long drive in our van until New Zealand, as the plan is to stay in Mumbai and sort out our Visas for NZ and arrange the shipping of our van, get our medicals etc. Quite a daunting task. To be honest we were not really looking forward to Mumbai as we were expecting another smelly, dirty, hectic and very expensive city, where we knew we were probably going to have to stay for at least two weeks. On the other hand, it was quite exciting because we knew this was one step closer to getting to New Zealand which is getting more exciting by the day.

The road this time, despite supposedly being the best in India and lined with toll booths, let down its reputation! It took us 10 hours to get to Mumbai which we expected to be just a short hop. It was a very pretty drive though, through quite a rural and very green, hilly part of India. We stopped off for lunch in a roadside "Dhaba"

which is always quite a fun experience. The
menu is quite often in Hindi and we really
have no idea what we are ordering - we just
pick things at random and see what we get!
The great thing is Rhona is feeling much better these days and is managing to eat cur-
ries and other spices quite regularly now -
phew!

Entering Mumbai felt sort of like entering
Glasgow - on a very big scale! We crossed the
bridge onto Mumbai Island, marking the
edge of the urban sprawl, and then passed
a sign saying 'Mumbai 53km'! The high-
ways into the city are brilliant and not too
crowded which is the most common problem in Indian cities. High-rises both fancy
and completely decrepit line the sky and
we were very excited to see the sea for the
first time in ages! In fact, we were so excited, that we nearly crashed the van into
the truck in front of us when it stopped in
traffic! Rickshaws are banned in the centre
of Mumbai and are replaced by hundreds of
black and yellow taxi cabs. Red buses, al-

most like London buses are also numerous.
It's crazy to say it, but in one of the biggest and busiest cities in the world, there is
a real sense of peacefulness. Modern shops
and coffee houses can be found everywhere,
which can be a refreshing taste of home
when needed. We have found the hustlers
and sellers a lot less pushy and in fact,
people generally leave you alone after you
say "no" once. The people are very friendly,
and will make pleasant chit chat without
ending with the words: "look at my shop".
We have spent our evenings so far meander-
ing along the seafront, enjoying the atmosphere with hundreds of locals, while horses
and carts decorated brightly speed along
the promenade.

Our first day here was a Sunday. We got
up quite early and made our way to the
train station for our first Indian railway experience. Because Sunday's are quiet we decided we'd try travelling second class, (20p
return for both of us), which on a week-
day would normally be packed tighter than

sardines. The trains here are super-efficient and leave so regularly you never need to hang around waiting. We jumped aboard the ancient carriage and sat on the metal bench seats. It was great fun. We love the way everyone just hangs out of the open doors when the train is moving even if there are loads of spare seats! Our stop was about 30 minutes away, where we had arranged to go to a church that friends back in Hastings are closely involved with. We felt so completely at home straight away! We were greeted by so many people as we walked through the door and the service was so lively and passionate! We spent the afternoon with the pastor and his wife and children which was really special and we would love to return again.

We spent the next day travelling across town for a meeting with the shipping agents, which was very successful. Everything is under control in that department, and shipping our van should now be relatively easy. The day after that we had our medical inspections performed which we need for our New Zealand visa applications. That was fine and we should be getting our certificates in a few days. At one point we were approached by a man on the street and asked to be extras in a Bollywood movie in the making, which we thought would be a fantastic laugh. However, it was a full 12 hour day and happened to clash with our medicals! Bummer!

It's also pretty amazing how, though highly illegal, we get offered marijuana and cocaine, almost as often as taxi's! The red light district is listed as "must-see", "women at work for so many years!" tourist attraction by taxi drivers along with all the other temples and historic sites.

Our map of Mumbai isn't very good, and we've managed to get lost the couple of times we were driving the van. The best was when we ended up in the middle of a large bazaar market! It took us ages to push our way out of it again through throngs of people. It was great to see though, and we didn't have the hassle of trying to walk past all those stalls without buying anything!

Following that, we got a bit of bad news, in that we've found out that once we've submitted our application for visa's they take between three and twelve weeks to be processed! This changes our plan once again, and could possibly make things very tight for Simon getting to NZ in time for his course starting, not to mention being in India without our passports for all that time. So we are not completely certain what our next plan is, but we will probably be in India for another four weeks and possibly will visit the south as originally planned, whilst waiting for our visas. Our van can only be shipped once we leave India (something to do with customs), and so we will still have our transport. The shipping agents can make instant arrangement to put the van in its container and seal it for sending as soon as we have our plane tickets to NZ.

We decided to do a bit more sightseeing

around Mumbai to take our minds off the complications and took a small passenger ferry to 'Elephanta Island' about an hour's boat ride away. There aren't actually any elephants there but some ancient caves and temples carved into the cliff face. It felt like we were in an Indiana Jones movie, walking into these huge rock-cut pillared caves. They were truly enormous and had huge carvings of various gods and other creatures all over the inside walls. Quite spectacular. We also walked up to the top of the hill where they had two huge old war-time cannons to protect the harbour. They were joined together by long underground passages and rooms, and if we had thought to bring a torch then we probably could have made it through all the tunnels from one to the other!

We have now decided that it is not a good idea to submit our visa applications in India, it seems to be possible to do it after we arrive in New Zealand on visitors visas, where we can be a lot more relaxed about it. So with that decided, we are now going ahead and putting the van on the next available ship, and flying the relatively short hop across to Singapore. We have had another meeting with our shipping agents, and have booked our flights for Thursday the 31st of July, and the van will be departing on 3rd of August. We'll still spend a couple of weeks relaxing around Singapore and going to a stunning island off the coast of Malaysia, before catching a plane from Singapore on the long haul down to Auckland. we'll wait until then to update the blog further, so unless we run into some complications, the next time you hear from us we should be in New Zealand and mission accomplished! Here's hoping!

Mileage: 10,919

Days on the road: 92

Temperature range: 27 to 34 deg C

Elepahanta Island, Mumbai

SINGAPORE & MALAYSIA

Tuesday, 12th
August 2008

"Selamat tengah hari!"

In our last week in Mumbai, we found out more than ever, that India is a very manic place, and Mumbai is possibly the most manic place in India! This coupled with trying to sort out all sorts of things that would have been hard for us in our own country; we had a very stressful last week! We were up late the night before we were due to fly to Singapore, going in and out of internet cafes, our shipping agents' office, and trying to courier documents back home. Basically our bank (Barclays) refused to let us transfer any money unless we actually went into a branch in the UK which was obviously not possible! Thanks to our great parent agents back home, we were able to sort it out though and we managed to fit in a fine curry on our last night as well.

So we waved goodbye to Indian roads, Indian driving, dirt, taxis (that you can't fit into!), and smells, and got on our lovely Singapore Air Boeing 777. Arriving in Singa-

pore from India must be one of the biggest
contrasts ever! We were amazed by what
felt like the smoothest roads, most cour-
teous driving, cleanest streets, and fanciest
buildings we had ever seen! Our hotel was
in the 'red light' district as that is where the
cheapest hotels are and many locals seem
to think it is a terrible area, but we found it
to be quite pleasant with the coolest eating
scene in Singapore. Singapore is all about
shopping, and although we tried our best
not to be pulled in to it, we came away
with a few bits and bobs including a video
camera, so that's cool! Lovely city to wan-
der round anyway, being so clean and quiet
with heaps of classy waterside restaurants
and bars lining the river and coast. We only
spent one day there though before we shot
off by train and bus to our tropical island
paradise of Pulau Tioman in Malaysia. Here
we stayed for 9 days, and really became
complete beach bums! It was very beautiful indeed and a lovely strip of sand with
clear bright turquoise water and silky soft

sand. Lovely - we felt like we deserved it! Without making you go emerald green with envy, Simon went scuba diving down to an old wreck which was particularly exciting as we had bought a big triple set of famous five books, and had just been reading about the five looking for treasure on their wreck! He couldn't wait to get back to tell Rhona who was quite happy sunbathing. We stayed in a wooden chalet (shack) right on the beach, and it was just one step down onto the sand.

Back in Singapore, we are just counting down the hours until our flight leaves early in the morning, and that is where we are now, so we see you then!

Days on the road: 105

Temperature range: 27 to 32 deg C

NEW ZEALAND

Friday, 26th Sep-
tember 2008

"Kia Ora!"

Well without further ado, we can now proudly announce that we have officially driven from the UK to New Zealand in a van (with small cameo appearances from 2 big ships and a few aeroplanes), and our global challenge 'NZinavan' has successfully been completed!!! We arrived in a rainy Auckland in mid-winter on the 13th August 2008, exactly 15 weeks after we left Britain, and completely froze after having been in such hot places for so long!

Aside from the English Channel ferry crossing, we drove every inch of the way from humble Hastings in Britain, to the mighty metropolis of Mumbai in India. Our onward overland route was barred by political and beaurocratical (that's not a word) restrictions in Tibet and China meaning that we had to resort to using a ship to carry the van to New Zealand whilst we flew to meet with it again on the other side. Our trip has taken us across grassy plains, mountain passes, deserts and rivers, through forests, cities and villages, and past whole seas, tribes, nations and even continents. We have driven on 8 lane Autobahns, Pot-holed 'car-breaker' tarmac, 16th-century cobbles, dirt, sand dunes, mud, loose rocks, snow, and through sewerage pools as well as through crystal-clear mountain streams. The temperature has ranged from -2 to +47 degrees Celsius. We have stood under the baking Middle Eastern sun, just as we have the cascading Indian monsoon and the snow of Britain. We have delved 28 meters below sea level to the shores of the Caspian Sea, and up over 5200 meters in the Himalayas. We have crossed 95 degrees of longitude, 180 degrees of latitude, and have driven 11,500 miles. The most incredible thing is that the whole way, we never even got one flat tyre! The van just kept on going without even a hiccup. In fact, the only trouble we had was when 2 of the suspension leaves on one of the rear wheels snapped after bouncing over a mountain range continuously for 4 days (understandable). That was easily fixed, and the only other thing we did on the way was change the engine oil – once! We found it quite funny because we arrived in NZ and hired a car, and on the second day the tyre blew out!

From around the middle of Turkey onwards, the van started belching out black fumes from the exhaust pipe, especially at altitude, and going up hills. But that's just because (we discovered) the diesel in these places has around 200 times the amount of sulphur in it (and other nasties no doubt) as it does in Europe...and you wonder why they have poor air quality! When we were going through the dry dusty places (i.e. most of the way), emptying the air filter was almost a daily chore. This involved banging it against a wall until there is a sizeable pile of sand/dust on the ground, and you are completely powdered!

Rhona got pregnant the day before we left, yet she still managed to climb a 2500 metre ice-capped mountain in Slovakia, survived India in up to 47-degree heat with morning sickness, and took a rabies injection, antibiotics, and malaria tablets before we even found out! We figured that our baby must be extremely tough! Now Rhona is 23 weeks in and has a sizeable bump.

Sometimes the most memorable moments are the small things that make you laugh, cry, shiver or just think. Some of these might have seemed too small to put in the blog, so we have a few of them here. Indian Laundry is one such memory. Even if you stay in a hotel, what many might not realise is that when you give them your clothes and towels to wash, it is passed on to a laundry boy, who then takes it and hand washes it. This may be done in a private tub, but quite often it seems to go to either a large communal laundry pool or down to a river! It mostly came back crushed, a nice brown colour, and smelling distinctly of stale curry – lovely! Oh, how wonderful washing machines, irons and nice smelling detergent are!

One of Rhona's favourite experiences was all the really pretty clothes, jewellery, and colours we have experienced in many countries, especially Turkey and India. Also how people take real pride in their appearance even if they are just doing their daily chores. The aroma of the spice markets was wonderful with a whole display of interesting and very different ingredients.

For Simon one of the most shocking moments was using a urinal in a restaurant in Kathmandu, only to find out that it was in fact not plumbed in at all, it just emptied itself on the ground at his feet! Lovely!

As we're talking about toilets, there was another incident in Iran when we desperately needed to empty our portaloo. We passed a fuel station, which was under construction but appeared to have working toilets. There was nobody around so we snatched at the opportunity at last to empty our overflowing waste tank. As we poured away, we got that very satisfying feeling almost as though our sins were being washed away (they were particularly bad this time)! It wasn't until we had finished and properly cleaned it out that we realised that the foul-smelling semi-liquid had appeared oozing out of a bare pipe round the side of the block and had spread all over the building site! "Oops," said we, and planned to leave pronto (we weren't sure what punishments were dealt for such a crime in Iran). Just then, a truckload of builders arrived back from lunch, and started curiously inspecting the strange blue/green trickle with half-digested brown lumps and soggy paper that had mysteriously appeared in their building site! We said our "Salaam"s and cleared off!

Having just confessed that, we now actually have to say that among the worst discoveries we have made about the world would have to be the pollution. Something has got to be done about this. Ghastly (that's a good English word) at best, suffocating at worst, this just represents a dark stain of human pillage on the earth. It's all seemingly because governments are too interested in trying to become the next world superpower than to look after their own country and people.

Among the best discoveries is certainly the overwhelming power of humanity left in some people that would compel a person with nothing, to offer two dirty travellers with whom they have zero in common, everything they have without any want for a reward. It moves you to realise that this still exists, and hurts to wonder where this has gone in the western world.

We have seen many wonderful places on our travels, and have certainly been witness to some gloriously enchanting scenery, food, hospitality and culture. We didn't set off with any grand scheme in mind – we didn't even raise any money for charity (which was a bit lame), we just had an amazing chance to enjoy some of this planet that has been given to us, and we took it. We had

no idea what we would discover about this
world we live in, or ourselves if anything.
Maybe we would just come out of the other
side with more to offer? You may wonder if
we left the UK because we were searching
for something, but I think that this trip has
proved to us that we were not. If anything it
has shown us quite clearly that we have
everything we need because our God is
looking after us! The drive was good and all,
but it hasn't "opened our minds" or
"changed us forever" as some would claim.
It has mostly made us realise how privil-
eged we have been to have been born and
brought up in a country such as Britain.
We're not just talking about wealth here,
for one, Britain has world-class scenery:
walk around the rugged coast of Cornwall,
drive up the breath-taking Glen Coe in Scotland, and see the spotless beaches of Southern Wales. If you haven't been to these
places then go there, and you will know
that you have seen real beauty. We also realised that Britain has good food! From break-

fast right up to supper, this is the land of proper nosh – enjoy it! You can get fried breakfast or roast-beef-with-all-the-trimmings in other places, but it just ain't the same! As for historic marvels of architecture, just do a tour of Scottish castles; go see Stonehenge, or the tower of London – these all match up to the best of them in the world. When it comes to cities, you might think that the traffic is awful in British cities, but it really isn't! Nowhere else will you get the romance of walking down the high street of a city of a million people under a castle perched gloriously on a high crag above you than in Edinburgh. Nowhere else will you sample the grandness of Buckingham palace or the houses of parliament on your way to a U2 gig. As far as hospitality goes, well the other thing you just don't get anywhere else in the world is the welcome of a warm cosy pub where you can sit down in front of a fire to thaw out with a good pint that was brewed just down the road - aaaah! There is also nowhere in the world where

there is a coffee shop like Mr Beans! You can
enjoy all this without the constant worry of
disease-carrying mosquitoes, snakes and
other nasties. Consider all these things (and
we've not even started on public freedom),
and Britain a pretty good place!

We feel incredibly blessed to have been
able to do this trip, and have had an ace
time doing it, but we still think (in all ser-
iousness) that for us, the best of the world
is back home... that is until we got to New
Zealand... Wow this place is awesome!! We
left the rain of Auckland behind us and
headed down to Motueka in the Nelson region of the South Island where we will be
spending the next year and a half, and the
beauty just blew us away: calm translucent
water gives way to golden sands which in
turn rise up to snow-capped mountains all
around you. Every kind of outdoor activ-
ity imaginable is at your doorstep and is
the best in the world. We have already seen
the largest and clearest freshwater springs
in the world, seals giving birth, glorious

deserted beaches, stunning alpine scenery deep in snow, and all under a bright crystal-clear blue sky. The Nelson region has the highest amount of sunshine hours in the country and it is rare for two days to go by without one of them being glorious. We feel very at home here – we're enjoying rather British food (including great fish and chips), the scenery is quite Scottish-like, and so far people have been incredibly friendly and accepting towards us.

After finding a place to live and sorting out various things in Motueka, we headed back up to Auckland to wait for our van to arrive. This turned out to be a tormenting 3-week wait more than what we expected, and when our van finally did emerge from its dark box it had 6 weeks' worth of damp mould growing all over it and everything in it. The quarantine inspectors were about ready to send it the incinerator, but instead recommended that it be given the full deep steam cleaning treatment, everything short of dipping it in acid! Comments such

as "you should have left it in India", and
"is that a van?" were noted. We reminded
them of its glorious track record but didn't
want to displease the people whose deci-
sion it would be to let us have it back!
After it's embarrassing 'army bath', we took
it to the garage to get a Warrant of Fitness
(like an MOT), and the guy took one look
at it and basically said: "you must be jok-
ing!" Sure enough, one look at the underside
would make you believe that they dragged
it along the bottom of the ocean rather than
in 'containerised transport' by the amount
of rust it had developed. So, at that point,
we realised that it was not even near worth
spending any more money on it than we
had already spent getting it here, and we are
ending this story with our most stalwart
steed going to the scrap heap. What a disap-
pointment...not mention money down the
squat loo. It got here and completed the
mission, but we should have left it behind!

So now we are very much looking forward to staying in one place for a while. We

have found somewhere to live, Simons flying course is now underway, and the transition to our new start seems to have gone incredibly smoothly. On that note, we are saying "ta for now", and thank you so much to all the people who have read our blog and been so positive about it. We are especially thankful to those who have been praying for us.

We really appreciate it. It is safe to say that we have no doubt that it kept us going at times! Still, watch this space, there's talk of a hard copy of this, and who knows what we'll get up to next!

We will have more adventures, but that's another story!

The End

Total Mileage: 11500 miles

Days on the road: 142

New Zealand temperatures (Aug): -2 to 15 deg

New Zealand Diesel: £0.50

Geothermal reserve, Rotorua

Printed in Great Britain
by Amazon

48412540R00132